10856
.50
d

D1431512

320

John W. Sewill

THE METHOD OF FREEDOM

BY

WALTER LIPPMANN

THE METHOD

OF

FREEDOM

BY

WALTER LIPPMANN

*

New York

THE MACMILLAN COMPANY

1934

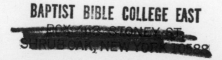

PRINTED IN THE UNITED STATES OF AMERICA
BY THE STRATFORD PRESS, INC., NEW YORK

For the privilege of delivering the Godkin lectures I am indebted to the President and Fellows of Harvard University.

To Mr. James Bryant Conant I owe the encouragement to undertake the work of preparing them.

Since this book is a tract for the times, it is perhaps desirable to date it by saying that I began to work on it during the summer of 1933, shortly after the conclusion of the first Roosevelt Congress and the adjournment of the World Economic Conference, and that the lectures were delivered at Cambridge, Massachusetts, in May, 1934.

W. L.

FOREWORD

THIS book is made out of lectures delivered at Harvard on the foundation established in memory of Edwin Lawrence Godkin. Those who are invited to give these lectures must deal with some aspect of "The Essentials of Free Government and the Duties of the Citizen."

Anyone who accepts an invitation of this sort in times like these cannot fail to realize that the essentials of free government are more seriously challenged than they have been for generations. It is this challenge that these lectures profess to meet. They are a statement of the principles by means of which, as I see it, a nation possessing a highly developed economy and habituated to freedom can make freedom secure amidst the disorders of the modern world. If that seems too bold a pretension, I can say only that the issue is joined and that those who would be free must make up their minds as to where they propose to go and how they propose to go there. The defense of liberty requires positive convictions and affirmative principles. It

cannot be conducted effectively by those who will
not examine candidly the reasons why the regime
of liberty is almost everywhere on the defensive,
nor by those who will not distinguish between the
traditional policies of free states in the Nineteenth
Century and the essentials of free government itself.

The things I have to say would have been mean-
ingless while Godkin was still alive. At the time of
his death in 1902 the issues with which we have to
deal were in the making but they had not been
precipitated. In the past twenty years, in the two
decades since the beginning of the Great War, they
have been precipitated. Yet I confidently believe
that while the principles set forth in these lectures
depart radically from the liberal programs which
Godkin expounded so eloquently, they are nevertheless consistent with the spiritual purposes of
which those programs were the transient expres-
sion.

For policies and programs are only instruments
for dealing with particular circumstances. Purposes
and ends embodying a conception of the good life
and of what makes for dignity in human existence
are older than all our working principles and will
survive them. And, therefore, he who would be
loyal to the end must in changing circumstances

be prepared to alter the means; even the gods on Olympus took diverse shapes when they walked on earth. So I do not believe that liberty is, as we have been told on high authority, a corpse. But neither do I believe it can live only or live forever in the body it inhabited during the Nineteenth Century. And it is in the conviction that freedom is finding a new incarnation in a new body of principles that these lectures have been written.

It is in the English-speaking countries chiefly that these new principles are being wrought out. They are being applied experimentally, not without confusion, hesitation, and contradictions. Nevertheless, in the maze of measures taken in the British Commonwealth and in the United States, and also in the Scandinavian countries, there is now discernible the pattern of a new social policy. It would work better if it were more consciously pursued, if it were disentangled from measures which cross it and neutralize it at many points. Yet it is working sufficiently well, I believe, to justify us in recognizing that there has appeared in the modern world a method of collective action which is indigenous to free nations with a highly developed capitalist economy.

It has been the fashion to try to discover the future of capitalism by studying countries where capitalism is primitive and the future of political institutions where liberty has no traditions. Yet one might as well go to Massachusetts to study the habits of the palm tree as go to Russia to learn about the prospects of modern capitalism or to Central Europe to learn about the evolution of representative government. It would seem reasonable to remember that in the English-speaking countries there are the oldest and most powerful of governments,—therefore, presumably, an aptitude among the people for the art of governing; that in these same countries wealth is more abundant than in any others, and that therefore, it is not likely that they are wholly lacking in the knowledge of how to conduct an economy.

I wish it had been possible for me to support these generalizations with detailed examination of the measures taken in the United States, Great Britain, Australia, Canada and Sweden, during the past decade. But it would have been physically impossible to assemble all the material or to digest it within the compass of these lectures. So I have ventured simply to state the general principles which appear to me to have animated the measures which show the greatest promise of restoring and maintaining order in a regime of liberty. The very last thing I should like to believe is that I had invented or discovered them and was expounding a private panacea. My highest hope would be to be able to say as Montesquieu did in *The Spirit of the Laws:* "I have not drawn my principles from my prejudices but from the nature of things."

CONTENTS

Part Three

GOVERNMENT IN A REGIME
OF LIBERTY

THE METHOD OF FREEDOM

PART ONE

REVOLUTION IN THE GREAT SOCIETY

I. THE UPHEAVAL OF PRIVATE EXISTENCE

DURING the rebellion of 1745 when the Pretender, Prince Charles Edward Stuart, invaded England with his Highlanders, David Hume was living in a country house near St. Albans. He was employed as the companion of a young nobleman. His charge, Lord Annandale, was amiable enough. But he was hopelessly insane, and the management of his estate had fallen into the hands of an incompetent and designing group of relatives and lawyers. Hume had accepted the post because he needed money and the leisure to go on with his philosophical writing; the last thing he had expected was that he would become involved in a complicated intrigue. Yet he stayed on with the mad Marquis. While the south of England was stricken with panic as Prince Charles moved forward unopposed into Derby, the philosopher and historian was engaged in thwarting the plots of his lordship's servants and retainers and was writing despairing letters to his friends about "the inhuman treatment we meet with here" which "throws me into the greatest melancholy."

One of his earlier biographers remarks that "there is perhaps nothing more curious in the whole dispute" about the affairs of Lord Annandale's household "than the indifference with which" the Stuart rebellion "fraught with so much importance to his countrymen, is spoken of by Hume." During the momentous struggle his thoughts appeared to have been occupied with a certain Captain Vincent whom he suspected of wishing to dominate the affairs of the Marquis. A more recent biographer explains away Hume's indifference to the crisis by pointing out that a Scotsman living in England would have been under suspicion during the Civil War and that elementary prudence would have compelled Hume to remain apart from the public events. Perhaps so. But there will have been many others who in their own way were almost entirely preoccupied with their personal affairs.

In the reconstruction of history, and even more in the projection of ideas which have the pretension to make history, there is no easier way to be misled than to forget how absorbing and tenacious is the private life of men. Only in a perspective that obscures the intimate actuality of things do events conform readily to the large historical patterns. "The whole," says Sainte-Beuve, "acquires after the event, a semblance of reason which is deceptive,"[1] and the more remote the period, and the less we can see of its detail, the more readily all the evidence conforms to the large generalizing principles. For it is in the countless realms of privacy that civilization is carried on. The life of mankind does not stop while great issues are being decided. That life goes on,—all about the public events, and in spite of them, endlessly through all the movements and crises, adventures and experiments that fill the conscious excited minds of men.

Were it not for these ultimate reserves of private habit, energy, and adaptability, the failures of the rulers of men would long since have proved to be irreparable. For it has not been the wisdom of rulers but the private persistence of men which has carried mankind through the crises of history and has preserved civilization even when institutions have collapsed. Thus it is that no ordinary wind blowing upon the surface of the waters can cause more than a momentary agitation of the deeps of human existence. The crises of politics are

[1] C. A. Sainte-Beuve *Causeries du Lundi*, on M. Guizot.

usually regarded by most men as theatrical spec-
tacles and sporting events. If they signify great
issues, their meaning is hidden. Their consequences
are deferred. To convulse the mass of the people
and draw them actively into public affairs, the impact of events must be direct and extensive upon
the realms of privacy. They must disturb drasti-
cally the common way of life, as when able-bodied
men are mobilized for war, or a city is sacked, or
whole communities devastated by catastrophe. Not
only must the effect penetrate private careers and
separate households; it must appear to transcend
private and customary remedies. It must, too, be
so long-continued and cumulatively provoking that
men lose hope of a natural return of their normal
expectations.

At such a juncture there is a major crisis in human affairs. Wholly new forces, churned up out of
the depths of human anxiety and bewilderment,
manifest themselves. Old principles fall into disre-
pute. The ruling classes and the established order
are impeached and can depend no longer upon the
habitual assent of the people. Then, as Burke said
in his *Thoughts on French Affairs*, there are dec-
larations of "*a new species of government*"; there
is "a revolution of doctrine and theoretic dogma."
Crises of this nature are not produced by the ordi-

nary mistakes of governments or by ordinary conflicts of interest among the people. For there is a profound inertia in the mass of men manifesting itself in a prejudice in favor of the known and the certain. Against willful interference, based on merely theoretical considerations, they can be counted upon to defend their established habits and beliefs. The reformer who deliberately lays hands upon existing institutions—upon altar, throne, flag, constitution or property,—because he has seen the vision of some greater good, is counted an alien, an impious disturber of the peace, and a sacrilegious enemy of the gods. Among the people, except in very extraordinary times, revolutionists are a small minority. It is only when established custom does not any longer work the expected results, when the whole organization of men's lives is in confusion, that a generally revolutionary condition exists. The people listen to unfamiliar ideas when their familiar routine has broken down.

We live in the midst of such a period of revolution. The things that were certain have become uncertain. What was normal is not reliable. Under these conditions those who were most dogmatic in the old faiths, once they have lost them, are most readily credulous of new faiths. The inertia of men, which in settled times makes for stubborn resistance to novelty, becomes a fatalistic acceptance of change; they surrender easily to the mere turmoil of affairs, and open the gates of the city to the first barbarian who comes demanding admittance in a sufficiently loud voice. In his assurance the crowd find a cure for their own uncertainties, in his assumption of authority a fixed point amidst their own bewilderment. This is the moment, too, when they listen most eagerly to the great generalizers who come to them announcing that they have identified the governing elements in human affairs: to a Karl Marx who undertakes to assure them, on the ground of his dialectic, that the struggle between capitalist and proletarian is the final conflict, that the issue is rigid, the result pre-determined, and that under communism men will "leap from the kingdom of necessity to that of freedom"; to an Oswald Spengler who with equal vehemence, but promising a different outcome, assures them, on the ground of his morphology of history, that "for us . . . our direction, willed and obligatory at once, is set for us within narrow limits . . . We have not the freedom to reach to this or that, but the freedom to do the necessary or to do nothing . . . a task that historic necessity has set *will* be accomplished with the individual or against him."

No one can deny that prophecies delivered in

this style are magnificent. But there will be many who, needing a political faith by which they can live, would prefer to found it not upon a grandiose reconstruction of the whole of human history but upon observation of existing conditions and such knowledge of the art of government as they are able to draw upon. They will agree with Burke that "the science of constructing a commonwealth, or renovating it or reforming it, is, like every other experimental science, not to be taught *a priori*." [1] And if this method appears "flat and vapid" to those who feel that "there must be a great change of scene; there must be a magnificent stage effect; there must be a grand spectacle to rouse the imagination, grown torpid with the lazy enjoyment of sixty years security," it can at least be said for it that in this temper and by this method the English-speaking peoples have wrought for themselves a not inglorious destiny and a not inconsiderable influence in the affairs of mankind.

2. THE FAILURE OF THE POST-WAR RECONSTRUCTION

The present mood of revolutionary change is very plainly not the product of propaganda and the

[1] *Reflections on the French Revolution.*

agitation of conscious revolutionists. In the western nations men have come reluctantly, and only under dire compulsion, to the opinion that the old order cannot be restored. When the war ended, the true desire of the mass of the people was made very plain: they wished to recover the peace, the plenty, and the liberties they had been denied during the four years of fighting. There were, to be sure, some revolutionary manifestations in almost all countries. But everywhere west of Russia they subsided quickly or were easily suppressed. By the year 1923, or thereabouts, the old order seemed to be re-established, and, for five or six years after that, discontent abated almost everywhere.

In the United States Mr. Coolidge and Mr. Mellon enjoyed unprecedented popularity. Their social outlook was not only pre-war; it antedated the whole era of Theodore Roosevelt and Woodrow Wilson, and was the most frankly conservative which had been expressed in America since the days of Mark Hanna. The people liked the Coolidge era while it lasted and would have liked nothing so much as to have it last forever. Nor was it only here that men thought they were choosing to return promptly to normalcy. In Great Britain there was, to be sure, a Labor Government, but it had no power and it manifested no will to exercise power.

Its socialist creed was not its program: such energies as it could muster it devoted to the promotion of international peace and the revival of free-trade capitalism. The French passed through a severe financial and political crisis, during which wealth was measurably redistributed by inflation, and the normal processes of government temporarily suspended. But when the operation was completed in 1926, the French people were more than ever firmly attached to the straightest orthodoxy. The Italians had a political revolution which abolished their civil liberties, but the concentrated power of the dictatorship was for the next years devoted to restoring and preserving the essential features of the pre-war capitalism. Even the Germans, who had been devastated by defeat, revolution, and inflation, had a revival in the late Twenties, and during this revival bolshevism and fascism alike became inconsequential. As for the Russians, it was in this era that Stalin overthrew Trotzky and turned from the crusade for a world revolution to the construction of a socialist regime within Russia.

It is, I believe, clear enough that the peoples have not been consciously disposed to overthrow and remake the social order. They were evidently content with it when it worked well enough to produce the standard of life to which they had become accustomed. They did not mean to disrupt it. They meant to preserve and develop it, and while that prospect existed, the popular judgment was conservative. The people proved again the truth of Burke's observation in his Letter to the Sheriffs that: "The bulk of mankind, on their part, are not exceedingly curious concerning any theories, whilst they are really happy; and one sure symptom of an ill-conducted state is the propensity of the people to resort to them." This, too, was the conclusion of Machiavelli,[1] when he said that there are few difficulties in preserving a state in which the people are "long accustomed to the family of the prince"; it is "sufficient only not to transgress the customs of the ancestors," that is to say to maintain the familiar standard of life and to fulfill traditional expectations.

It was the failure to achieve a restoration of the pre-war economy, rather than a conscious desire to remake it, that has brought on a general revolutionary condition in the western world. The summer of 1931 may be taken, I think, to have been the moment of transition from the past into the present. Between May and September of that year the post-war reconstruction collapsed. The collapse was marked by such outward signs as the inter-

[1] *The Prince*, Chapter 2.

national financial panic, the breakdown of the reparation and debt settlements, the destruction of the post-war gold standard, and the abandonment of the principles of free trade by the British. But these were only the spectacular evidences of a much deeper disorder amidst which the conviction was implanted in men's minds that the pre-war economy had not been successfully re-established because in fact it could not be.

We can now see, I think, why the post-war reconstruction was almost certain to fail. The old economy was a world-wide system of transactions that no one had deliberately contrived. It had grown to be what it was by the initiative, the compliance, the foresight and the miscalculation of multitudes of men in the course of many generations. It was not a consciously constructed organization, and it was therefore, by its very nature, unsuited to conscious control. It was particularly intractable to the only kind of control which men were organized to exert, that is to say, the control by separate, sovereign, popular governments.

The post-war decade brought into high relief the contradiction arising from the fact that as citizens men were organized under political governments in national states while as producers, consumers, debtors and creditors they belonged to a cosmopolitan economy. Their instruments of deliberate public action were national in scope; their vital interests were supra-national and eluded control. As members of the Great Society on which their fortunes depended, they were in a highly vulnerable position. Large populations needed food and raw materials supplied by producers who were bound to them only by a cash nexus and were separated from them by political frontiers. To pay for these necessities they had to have access to markets within the jurisdiction of foreign sovereignties. The flow of capital, which determined how and where and at what men should work, was directed by private calculations of risk and profit. In order to facilitate foreign trade and foreign investment an international monetary system had developed, and it had become the dogmatic duty of central bankers to maintain an international system of parities to which the national interest had to conform. All important movements in the price level anywhere, whether due to changes in the supply of gold and silver, or the demand for them, or the use of them as the base of credit, or to alteration in the ratio of costs to prices in large countries, had to be transmitted to all other countries within the system. These changes in the value of money imposed upon the people what amounted to a periodic redistribution of the national wealth, which had no relation whatever to their conscious national purposes.

Yet these very same people, who had so little power over their own economic fate, had become organized in powerful states. The contrast between the political independence of the western peoples and their economic dependence, between their national pretensions and their subjection to cosmopolitan forces, developed gradually in the century from Waterloo to Sarajevo. At the end of the Eighteenth Century the control which governments exercised over industry and commerce, in the interest of the landed classes, was vexatious and destructive; the liberation of the entrepreneur from this obsolete political control was rational and necessary. But the gospel of laissez-faire, which men treated as a revelation of the very nature of the universe, in fact reflected quite temporary conditions. The capitalist economy was undeveloped: the greater part of the population in all countries was still settled upon the land and was reasonably self-sufficient. Thus the early capitalism, though it soon produced great abuses in the treatment of labor, did not vitally implicate the whole mass of the people. There was therefore no overwhelmingly urgent demand that the capitalist economy should be controlled except in relatively minor ways. Moreover, the people who might have demanded control were pre-occupied with the effort to achieve political unity and political power. But by the end of the Nineteenth Century, capitalism had developed to a point where it involved the vital interests of whole nations, and democratic nationalism had developed to a point where the popular will, once it became articulate, was irresistible.

Sooner or later, gradually or violently, it was then certain that the political power of the masses would be used to defend and improve their economic position. When men achieve power, they will use it. They will use it to promote what they believe is their interest, and no abstract principle about the virtues of not using their power will long restrain them. The only thing which could and did restrain them, causing them to hesitate in the use of their power and to proceed moderately and gradually, was the success of the capitalist order in providing an immediate prosperity. Since the consolidation of popular power, laissez-faire capitalism has been like a man condemned who is reprieved repeatedly because he works miracles. The more the political state was democratized, the more imperative it was for private capitalism to give off continual prosperity. Laissez-faire had come to mean: Let them show us. It had no deeper attachments in the moral habits of the people. Private capitalism was allowed to proceed without radical interference as long as it could produce a rising standard of life for the mass and profitable careers for the more energetic and talented individuals. Its legal rights, its philosophical justification, its theoretic defenses, its record of achievement, were imposing; but, with power diffused in the mass, these buttresses were in fact hollow. Since the democracies have become conscious of their strength, the private capitalism of the Nineteenth Century has been a kind of tolerated anomaly. Shrewd conservatives have known that. They have known that the price of toleration was prosperity. In 1896 it was the full dinner pail. By 1928 the price had risen. It had become the two-car garage.

A social order, which does not command the moral loyalty of its people, which is sustained not by their convictions but by their satisfactions, is inherently unstable and unreliable. It depends upon an uncertain delivery of material benefits and not upon genuine attachment to the commonwealth; upon bread and circuses, in fact, and not upon a settled communion. Revolution is endemic, and the social order is at the mercy of events.

3. THE RETREAT FROM CHAOS.

We shall never know how the anomalies of free capitalism and political democracy would have worked themselves out had the issues not been precipitated by the World War. In a few months the accepted principles of Nineteenth Century capitalism were abandoned. Each state seized the control of that part of the cosmopolitan economy which lay within its frontiers or within reach of its army and navy. For the regulating mechanism of the markets, of private profits, of the gold standard, and of the movements of capital, there were substituted managed, rigorously centralized, national economies. Prices were fixed. Supplies were rationed. Labor was conscripted. Capital was allocated. Production was directed. Excess profits were confiscated. By blockade and embargo the fabric of the world's markets was torn to pieces. Within two or three years a highly militarized form of planned and regimented state socialism was set up all over the western world. The separation of political and economic power, which was the cardinal tenet of the old order, was suddenly and swiftly abolished.

It was supposed at the time that the war was

merely an episode, that the eggs which had been scrambled would be unscrambled when peace was restored. The state socialism of the war was to be dismantled. An attempt was made to do this. The attempt failed. It failed because the war controls had not merely suspended the operation of the pre-war economy. They had radically dislocated it.

Markets that had been closed by blockade did not reopen. New vested interests had been established and they pre-empted the markets. Nations, which had suffered for lack of food and raw materials, had become more self-sufficient. The volume, the kind, the origin and the destination of exports and imports had been altered, and with this the capacity and the need of each country to buy and sell what it formerly bought and sold. In each country there had been inflation,—but in different degree. Thus the relation of costs to prices was altered, the old parities of exchange were destroyed, and each country was compelled to make its own decisions as to how far it could, would, or must deflate.

The Great Society had been cut into parts, and among the parts some had shrunk and some had swelled, some had been lost and some had been replaced from new designs. The mere removal of the war controls did not cause the fragments to come together again; they no longer fitted one another. Thus the self-regulating and self-adjusting character of the old order had been destroyed. It was operated by a multitude of private transactions, and was kept in a working equilibrium by continual, as it were, interstitial adjustments and at reasonably long intervals by drastic liquidation of accumulated errors. For the individual these adjustments were feasible when they were small and infrequent and on the fringes of an immense routine. His decisions dealt with modest issues in a familiar environment; the road was not straight and one had to watch the turns, but a prudent man following time-honored conventions could stay on it.

The war dislocated affairs so much that they were no longer manageable by the kind of effort which ordinary men engrossed in their interests were capable of making. Then the interdependence of the Great Society was seen to be not a rational co-operation but the fortuitous concourse of individual efforts undertaken without direction or a common view of the whole. Sir Arthur Salter has described it well when he says that "the economic and financial structure under which we have grown up was at the moment of its greatest perfection more like the marvelously intricate structures built by the instincts of beavers or ants than the deliberately designed and rational works of man." Its cohesive principle was not design but routine, and therefore, the economy could continue to work only if instinct and habit were not baffled by more than a modest minimum of the unexpected and the unfamiliar.

Though many people hoped and believed that the world would relapse into normalcy, the wiser statesmen and their financial advisers saw almost at once that the pre-war economy could not be restored merely by dis-establishing the war socialism. The restoration had deliberately to be undertaken as a matter of conscious policy. It was undertaken. Between 1922 and 1928 the central banks and the international financiers co-operated in the reconstruction of what they believed to be the old cosmopolitan capitalism. They worked under enormous, in fact under insuperable handicaps. For, although they had control over money and credit, they had almost none over commercial policy. By 1928 they had set up again an international gold standard and had stimulated a free movement of liquid capital. But production and trade, which had been dislocated by the war and driven into new channels, did not follow this financial leadership. They remained obstinately nationalistic in the midst of the cosmopolitan financial restoration. Thus the bankers and financiers found themselves operating the mechanism of money and credit according to theories which did not conform to the practices of industry or the policies of government. The accounts would not balance, and the reconstruction broke down.

. Conceivably it might have succeeded had the peoples been willing to keep their hands off and to refrain from exerting control at various points. But to have expected that, as most of us did, was to misunderstand the political realities. The people would gladly have seen capitalism revive and produce prosperity. They proved that by their votes between 1920 and 1928. But at the same time they held fast to the idea that they must never again be at the mercy of such an anarchy of senseless brutish forces as had prevailed in the war and just after it. Against that they were determined to defend themselves with the political power they knew they possessed. There was, then, a pervasive conflict in the public mind throughout the post-war decade. On the one hand, the people listened politely, at times with a mild enthusiasm, to the official and prevailing opinion that with some contriving, and some co-operation, the consequences of the war could be liquidated and the old economy restored. When there was evidence of restoration they approved. But the whole business was suspect. The people did not really trust these projects. They did not believe in the Great Society which had brought forth the war. They did not love their enemies or even their allies. The Great Society seemed to them too vast and too intractable to be governed as a whole rationally. As an unconscious collaboration it had worked till it was disrupted. But as a deliberate form of co-operation it required the meeting of too many minds and the consent of too many wills.

Their experience in the war suggested to them that the sacrifices which these international projects called for might be vain, that they dared not disarm, that they dared not trust for their own security to the benevolence of others, that they dared not open their markets or give up their claims or hand over to aliens, to distant institutions and for abstract considerations, anything they could use in controlling their own destiny.

Confronted with chaos in the Great Society as a whole, men retreated into the smaller societies with which they were familiar, convulsively insisting that in them they would establish for themselves oases of order and well-being. Of course the more they did this, the more they dislocated the Great Society itself; their separatism became the most active agent in producing the evils against which separatism seemed the only practical defense. There were eloquent voices raised to summon the people to the kind of co-operation which the restoration of the world economy seemed to require. These voices went unheeded. Not only had the bitter experience of the people taught them to doubt whether the pre-war order could be restored, but it had taught multitudes to feel that it ought not to be. Why make sacrifices to restore a thing which had proved to be so catastrophically vulnerable? Was that an ideal for which it was worth taking the awful risks of exposing themselves again to another calamity as immense as the one they had suffered? The devil take the liberals, the pacifists, the internationalists, the economists, the bankers and all the rest of those who had nothing better to offer than a return to the system under which millions had been killed and more millions still had been starved, stunted and frustrated. When the old order seemed actually to be returning during the latter years of the Twenties, this radical questioning was stilled. Prosperity covers a multitude of sins. But the questioning never died out, and when the prosperity collapsed, the rebellion became insistent all over the world, insistent in proportion to the suffering and the despair of the different nations.

It is above all other things security that the people are seeking. They have lived dangerously for twenty years, and the elementary instinct to survive is aroused. This is the energy of their discontent, and so great is it that it will crush anything which seems to stand in the way of relief from the intolerable disturbance of their lives. Principles, constitutions, rights, liberties, all these things are as nothing compared with their overwhelming passion to make secure again the peace of human privacy. This is the instinct to which every leader of men today appeals. He will make them safe. He will defend them from their enemies abroad and at home. He will master for them or show them how to master the turmoil of events in which they are caught. The separatism of nations and regions, of classes and races is the action of men fiercely seeking their own security amidst forces which appear to them alien and hostile. The surrender of liberty, the disenchantment with democracy, the revival of autocracy, are all manifestations of the same desire: that amidst chaos there shall be organized power to defend them. There is a method in their madness. The world economy having ceased to be self-adjusting, men everywhere are bent upon establishing what controls they can within the orbit of their powers. Somehow or other they are determined to

make a social order which will not be, as was the
Great Society of the pre-war world, so unmanageable and so vulnerable.

4. THE END OF LAISSEZ-FAIRE

In venturing to interpret the revolutionary impulse of the peoples as a passion for private security
in the midst of public disturbance I have intention-
ally sought what might be called its lowest common
denominator. That the impulse manifests itself in
one place as communism, in other places as fascism,
here as the New Deal, in many countries as measures of relief and restoration without a spectacular
name, makes it all the more necessary that we
should attempt to comprehend what it is at the
bottom that is moving men in their public actions.
For it is upon the ruling rather than the accidental
passions of men that a political faith should be
founded. Thus it is certain that men must eat; it
does not follow that they can eat only what the
cook chooses to provide. It is certain that most men
and women will marry; it is not certain that they
must marry a particular spouse. By the same token,
it was certain that after the breakdown of Czarism
there would have to be a new regime in Russia; it
was perhaps certain that it would have to be a strong

centralized regime. Yet it was not certain that it had to be the regime of the Five Year Plan. That was the dinner the cooks happened to provide for hungry men. After the collapse of 1932–1933 a New Deal of some sort was imperative. But not everything that has been dealt out was imperative. That has depended upon the temperament, the prejudices, the quick judgments of the dealers.

When, therefore, we accept the current saying that this crisis marks the end of laissez-faire, we must be ready to recognize that there are many possible alternatives to laissez-faire. Until we have explored them and chosen among them, the mere announcement that laissez-faire is dead gives us no clue whatever as to the best course for the future. In fact, we cannot proceed very far until we have made up our minds just what we mean by saying that laissez-faire is dead.

The pure doctrine of non-intervention in production and trade has never in fact been practiced anywhere. Even Adam Smith, let alone John Stuart Mill,[1] recognized exceptions to the rule. One could go further, I believe, and argue plausibly that most men have shown in their behavior that they wished to impose free capitalism on others and to escape it themselves. Employers have be-

[1] *Cf. Principles of Political Economy*, Bk. V, Chap. 11.

lieved in it for their employees, and have appealed to it against factory laws and unionism. But they have not hesitated to call upon the state for protection against foreign competitors. Manufacturers who had to ship goods have not hesitated much about regulating the railroads. In the past forty years, through trusts, mergers, combines, holding companies and cartels, men have gone to great lengths to limit, and where possible to abolish free competition.

There is no reason to think that business men under capitalism have had any consistent conviction in favor of laissez-faire. Their employees have certainly not had it. They have voted for tariffs when they were told their jobs depended upon them. They have voted to close the labor market by restricting immigration. They have voted for labor laws and they have organized unions. Like their employers they have believed in laissez-faire for others. So when the cost of living was high, they have joined in the outcry against monopolies and the extortions of the tariff. The farmers have been no more consistent in their devotion to free competition. They have demanded agricultural tariffs and have fought industrial tariffs. They have opposed monopolies that fix prices and they have sought credit and other forms of assistance to fix their own prices. Not even the bankers have been consistent. They have, until very recent times at least, assumed that capital invested in backward countries was under the protection of the navy, that the maintenance of spheres of influence for investments abroad was one of the principal duties of the State Department, and Mr. Coolidge, though he had the strongest convictions against governing, once tried to lay down the extraordinary rule that the Fourteenth Amendment had to be applied on Mexican soil.

In a realistic view of the old capitalism, it is not far from the truth to say that free competition existed in so far as men were unable to abolish it. The political history of the Nineteenth Century is in considerable part the record of the struggle of various interested groups to carve out for themselves areas in which competition was limited for their own advantage. It cannot be said, therefore, that the change through which we are passing is from laissez-faire to intervention by the state.

There was persistent intervention in the past. There was no laissez-faire where men were able to overcome it. In reality there was laissez-faire only in respect to the operation of the system *as a whole*. This is the point which marks the present transition. The new thing is not the amount, or the pervasiveness, or the rigor of government action, but its purpose. In the pre-war era the state intervened continually to assist or to protect private interests. Sometimes it was moved by humanitarian sympathies. Oftener it was moved by the pressure of organized groups. But whether it acted to remedy an abuse or to confer a privilege, its action was always, so to speak, marginal and incidental. The state assumed no responsibility for the operation of the economy as a whole. Since 1914 the state has become charged with that new and unprecedented responsibility. Capitalism has become so complicated that private initiative is insufficient to regulate it; the democratization of political power has made collective initiative imperative. There is, therefore, a new view of the state and of the economic order. The novelty is not that there is government intervention. That there has always been. Of that there might have been much more without marking any decisive change. The novelty is that the state is now compelled to look upon the economy as a national establishment for which it is responsible and not as a mere congeries of separate interests which it serves, protects and regulates.

This is, as Burke said, "a new species of government" in which the assumptions of laissez-faire have given way to the assumptions of collectivism.

5. MR. HOOVER AND MR. ROOSEVELT AS WITNESSES

The best witnesses to the irresistible character of this revolutionary change in the function of the state are those who in principle deplore it and yet have acted to carry it out. We need look no further than to our own history in the past five years.

When the post-war boom collapsed in 1929, the national government was in the hands of conservatives. They had won the elections of 1928 by a great majority. They had promised the people a continuation of prosperity and the very minimum of government interference. President Hoover himself was a convinced believer in the doctrine which he had called "rugged individualism." The country would gladly have re-elected Calvin Coolidge; it was profoundly reassured to know that Mr. Mellon would continue to be the Secretary of the Treasury; it believed in a policy of benevolent non-intervention in the operation of private enterprise. An observer of the American scene up to the month of October 1929 would, therefore, have felt justified in concluding that America had entered the golden age of laissez-faire capitalism.

Yet instantly when the speculative bubble burst, President Hoover felt it his duty to call together

the leaders of industry and of labor for the purpose
of taking collective action to avert depression. In
the next month Mr. Hoover exacted promises to
maintain prices, wages, and employment, to enlarge
capital investment, to increase public works, to establish a truce between capital and labor. There was
no legislation. The whole collective effort was to
be voluntary; there was felt to be no need for
compulsion since everyone agreed that it was the
self-evident policy to adopt. It was, however, a
national policy, initiated by the government and
imposed upon industry and backed by public opinion, and its purpose was to maintain prosperity in
the economy as a whole.

No better proof could be found of how thoroughly the consciousness of men had become im-
bued with the idea that the task of insuring continuity in the operation of the capitalist order is a
public responsibility. Although the President himself, his chief advisers, and the great majority of
the industrialists who conferred with him would,
in an academic discussion, have celebrated the virtues of laissez-faire and of individualism, in practice, faced with a real emergency, they turned as a
matter of course to collective action. They did not
merely reject the classic doctrine of liquidation
and individual readjustment after a boom; they

acted as if they had never heard of it. It did not occur to Mr. Hoover, who had preached the philosophy of individualism, to follow the example of Cleveland in the depression of the Nineties, of Grant in the Seventies, of Buchanan in the Fifties, of Van Buren in the Thirties or of Monroe in the Twenties. They had thought it no part of their duty, and not within their power, to take charge of the economy and direct it through the storm. Mr. Hoover regarded it as his obvious duty to take charge and to direct.

To this conception of the government's duty he adhered throughout his term. At the end, when he was fighting for re-election and seeking to warn the country against the collectivist spirit of the New Deal, Mr. Hoover's defense of his own Administration consisted in reciting the long list of things he had done to stop deflation and liquidation and to restore the working balance of the economy. It was an impressive list. He had spent billions in protecting banks, insurance companies and railroads against bankruptcy. He had spent great sums to maintain the prices of wheat and cotton. He had spent great sums on public works. He had striven to maintain wage rates. He had attempted to inflate credit. In pointing to his record, he did not say that he was an individualist who had let individuals make their own readjustments. He pointed with pride to the collective measures which he had taken to save individuals from making individual readjustments. He did not say he believed in laissez-faire and so had let nature, or the law of supply and demand, take its course. On the contrary, he insisted that he had done everything humanly possible to circumvent and overcome the impact of natural law in the business cycle.

Between Mr. Hoover and Mr. Roosevelt there was, in 1932, no issue of fundamental principle as to the responsibility of the modern state for the modern economy. Both of them recognized the responsibility. They differed as to how it could best be discharged, but not on the underlying question as to whether the attempt ought to be made to discharge it. Indeed it may be said that every major move made by Mr. Roosevelt was in principle anticipated by Mr. Hoover. Both of them used the nation's credit in an effort to relieve debtors and restore the equilibrium of prices. Both of them gave subsidies to agriculture. Both tried to control production. Both of them tried to maintain or to raise wages in order to enhance purchasing power. Both of them tried to stop "cutthroat" competition. Both of them resorted to public works. Both of them quarrelled with Wall Street,

with the stock market, with the investment bankers. Both of them resorted to protection against
world deflationary forces. Both of them made ten-
tative efforts to revive international trade. Mr.
Hoover tried to do virtually everything that Mr.
Roosevelt did in his first year. He moved more
cautiously; he applied smaller doses of the medi-
cine; he timed the doses differently, and he worked
against constantly mounting political opposition.
He was less lucky and he was less effective. But on
the point which concerns us here, which is that
laissez-faire is dead and that the modern state has
become responsible for the modern economy as a
whole, Mr. Hoover is the best of all witnesses. For
he acted on a doctrine which he professed to reject. There could be no better evidence of the degree to which the new doctrine is established.

6. THE OBLIGATION OF THE MODERN STATE

"Opinions," says P. Bayle, "are not the rules
for actions, and men do not follow them in their
conduct. The Turks believe in Fatalism and Pre-
destination, and yet they flee from danger just as
the French who do not have such a belief." [1] In

---

[1] Quoted in P. Sorokin, *Contemporary Sociological Theories*,
p. 544.

modern times, even those who believe in the fatalism of laissez-faire, have fled from danger as if they had no such belief. For the danger has been a real one and every responsible man has had to recognize it. On the one hand the modern economy has become infinitely complex; on the other, the democracy has become increasingly conscious of its power: the conjuncture of the two has rendered obsolete the concept of a neutral government.

The classic theory of the business cycle recognizes the fallibility of individual judgments, and holds that periodic depressions are the necessary correction of the accumulated misjudgments of the previous era of prosperity. This is not a bad description of what happened in the business cycles of the Nineteenth Century. But, if it is proposed to treat the theory as a guide to policy in the future, it is a dangerous one. It leaves out of account the rise of democracy with all that that involves in the way of resistance and activity on the part of the masses of the people. As long as democracy was unconscious of its power, it was possible to let hard times be the purge of previous mistakes. But with democracy become active, there can no longer be a fatalistic acceptance of the purge. The debtor, threatened with the loss of his home, the worker thrown out of his job, the depositor, threatened with the loss of his savings, are not willing to go through the purgation. They fight back. They will, if necessary, overturn the government and the social order when their own security is destroyed.

Thus it has come about that under modern conditions the state is compelled to intervene. It has to prevent the purge from taking place. The modern state has to prevent unemployment. It has to protect the standard of life of its people. This compels it to assume a responsibility which it has never yet attempted to discharge before the era in which we are living. The task of insuring continuity of the standard of life for its people is now as much the fundamental duty of the state as the preservation of national independence. All the other duties of the state, the preservation of national unity, the maintenance of law and order, the protection of liberty, and the administration of justice, have now become entangled with and contingent upon this new obligation to maintain what Mr. Douglas Copland has called the "continuity of an ordered life." [1] If the state fails to do that, its independence is threatened, as we can see in the case of Austria; its national unity is imperilled, as we can see almost everywhere in the exacerbation

[1] Douglas Copland, *Australia in the World Crisis 1929–1933.*

of separatist tendencies; law and order collapse as we can see in the extraordinary spectacle, unknown since the Renaissance, of large private armies mobilized in modern states; liberty is threatened, as we can see in all of Europe east of the Rhine.

The modern state cannot endure unless it insures to its people their standard of life. Only by making its people economically secure can a modern government have independence, wield influence in the world, preserve law, order, and liberty. That is now the central task of government, the very heart of statesmanship, the very essence of the present phase of what F. S. Oliver calls the endless adventure in the art of governing men.

PART TWO

THE CHIEF ALTERNATIVES IN THE ECONOMIC ORDER

THE great issues of modern statecraft turn upon the manner in which the state discharges its obligation to the people for their standard of life. There are no longer many responsible believers in the neutral state. No one seriously challenged President Hoover or President Roosevelt when they made it the premise of their policies that it is the duty of the government to promote recovery. No one has said very confidently, or obtained much of a hearing if he did say it, that this is not the government's affair and that the trouble must be cured by private initiative and private adjustments alone. It is in this sense that one may declare that laissez-faire is dead and that the collectivist principle is now generally accepted. The great issues of the contemporary world, as between conservatives and progressives, fascists, communists, and social democrats have to do with the kind of collectivism, how it is to be established, in whose interests, by

37

whom it is to be controlled, and for what ends. But about the underlying premise of all these policies, which is that the continuity of an ordered life is a collective responsibility, there is no debate.

It is when the premise is accepted that the real debate begins. The issues of that debate can be clarified, I believe, by distinguishing two radically different forms of collectivism. In practice neither of them exists anywhere in its pure and rigorous logical simplicity. Nor is it likely to. For all social orders are in fact hybrids of many principles. But it may nevertheless be useful to distinguish clearly the differences of pure principle so that in the choice of actual policies we may have a mark by which to take our bearings. And since, in order to discuss ideas, it is convenient to give them names, I shall call one the system of a Directed Economy, or Absolute Collectivism, and the other the system of a Compensated Economy, or Free Collectivism.

I. THE PRINCIPLES OF A DIRECTED ECONOMY

If we use the term collectivism to mean the assumption by the state of responsibility for the operation of the national economy *as a whole*, it may be said that modern collectivism began as a war measure. It was as a corollary of the mobilization, for the purpose of supplying the armies and sustaining the civilians, that the government took charge of the whole economy and dealt with it as a national establishment. The World War was a gigantic collectivist enterprise. The plans which were imposed upon production and trade were worked out in war colleges and war councils. They were enforced by military law. All the belligerents resorted to collectivism during the war. But in the countries where the consequences of the war were most irreparable, where the old order was most deeply devastated, that is to say in Europe east of the Rhine, military collectivism has perpetuated itself as communism, as fascism in several different forms, and as dictatorship.

It was during the period of civil war and foreign intervention that the Communist Party in Russia was transformed from a group of successful insurrectionists into a governing class, that the Red Army was created, and the conception of a planned economy imposed upon the Russian mind. In the pre-war literature of socialism the idea of a planned economy may have been adumbrated; there may be faint indications of it in the writings of Karl Marx and in the early works of Lenin. But it is not explicit, and it is not understood to be as it is today, the governing principle of the socialist order.

There is good reason to think that the communists were driven to planning as the capitalist nations were driven to planning: that is to say by military necessity. There are some students of Russia who argue with a show of evidence that the skeleton of the famous Five Year Plan was obtained by the communists from a project worked out by the Czarist General Staff for the purpose of making Russia self-sufficient in war. In any event, there can be no doubt that communism in practice originated in war and is pervaded with the spirit, the procedures, and the formations of military life.

The fascist type of collectivism is even more obviously a militarization of the civilian order. Fascism begins as a political party which soon becomes a private army, carrying arms, wearing its own uniform, sometimes flying its own flag. When the fascist army conquers the state, the law which it imposes upon the nation is the military law of unquestioned obedience to commands from the hierarchy of officers at the top.

The military pattern is the basic pattern of any directed social order. If a multitude of people is to act according to a definite plan, it must be militarized. That is to say: centralized decision must replace distributed decisions. There must be a hierarchy of officers, or, if you like, officials, and a rank and file of privates. The officers must command. The privates must obey. In place of argument, persuasion, bargaining, and compromise among individuals, there must be orders and the disciplined acceptance of those orders. It is inconceivable that among multitudes the free choice of individuals could be brought into agreement upon a comprehensive plan, or that a multitude of individuals who were free to co-operate or to stand apart could voluntarily carry out a national plan. If the social order is to be planned, it has to be directed as it is in war time, and the liberty of private transactions has to give way to regimentation.

In an economy which is directed according to a plan and for definite national objectives, the official must be superior to the citizen and the hierarchy of officials who compose the government must be absolute as against the individual. The citizen is a conscript; in principle his life is dedicated to the state, in practice it is dedicated to the officials who issue his orders to him. The law is the will of the rulers above him. They are subject to no law. There are no customs, contracts, constitutions, or ancient usages which limit them. His rulers are controlled only by their own judgment and by the scope of their own power.

In war time this monopoly of absolute power

rests upon physical force and patriotic feelings. If it is to be perpetuated when the emergency is passed, popular assent has to be created. That requires to begin with an absolute censorship on information and opinion and the complete abolition of all freedom of discussion. But that is not enough. There must be positive assent if the multitude is to execute the plans of its rulers. It is necessary, therefore, to indoctrinate the people with the official view. An absolute state monopoly of news, propaganda, education and culture is required. Nothing must be known to the people which might cause doubt or disloyalty. Nothing must be uttered that might disturb them. They must be overwhelmed. They must be drilled. They must be stuffed with the official view of all things, of all contemporary events, of the past, of the future, of the constitution of the universe and the providence of God.

An iron discipline is needed to make millions of people behave according to a plan. They do not naturally co-ordinate themselves properly. Absolutism is not merely incidental to a directed economy in its early phases. It is the basic principle of a directed economy. It is only by abolishing freedom of choice in the disposal of labor and income and savings that production can be directed ac-

cording to a unified plan and the supply of all
things brought into perfect adjustment with the
demand for them. Thus, if there is freedom to
choose an occupation, there is no likelihood whatever that everyone will choose just that occupation which fits the plan. Under freedom there will
be over-crowding in some occupations and lack of
manpower in others. Successful planning is even
more impossible where men have freedom to
choose what they will buy, that is to say, freedom
to determine what kind of life they will make for
themselves out of the products of their labor. For
then the planner must make guesses about the preferences of the people, and he might guess wrong.
This problem does not arise in a country like Russia where the population is so poor that practically
all income has to be spent on the obvious necessities of existence. Since the demand for staples is
greater than the supply, the producer can sell what
he makes. But once a people has risen above the
level of subsistence to the level where it has income
to spend for comforts and luxuries, the caprices of
individual taste become extremely disconcerting
to the planning commissioners. It is best, therefore, under a directed economy to keep private incomes to a subsistence level, and to let the state
spend the surplus on such collective pleasures and

luxuries as it may in its wisdom deem it desirable to offer the people.

This is the logic of absolute collectivism, of a planned and regimented economy. It is hardly necessary to say that not even a band of complete fanatics could follow this logical pattern to its full conclusion. The human material remains refractory. There are limits beyond which it is not possible to drive even the most abjectly terrorized population. There is a limit to what ruthless determination can achieve. But we should have no illusions as to the essential character of an economy which is directed according to a unified plan. When we see visions of the great abundance which we could all theoretically enjoy if we turned over the whole economic order to a general staff of technicians to run on the highest engineering principles, with all waste and friction abolished, with everything carefully calculated as part of a comprehensive plan, let us have no illusions about the violence with which the technicians would have to suppress the contrariness of free men.

It is no accident that wherever and whenever planned collectivism has been instituted, in all countries during the war, in the post-war dictatorships, it has required censorship, espionage, and terrorism to make it work. What else can one expect? How else, except by suppressing the liberties of individual men, is the will of the officials to prevail without let or hindrance from the wills of individual men?

2. THE PRINCIPLES OF A COMPENSATED ECONOMY

It is often assumed in current discussion that all the nations must make an exclusive choice between the old theoretically neutral state on the one hand and some form of absolute collectivism and a directed economy on the other. The militant partisans have done their best to narrow the choice to these alternatives. Yet there exists a radically different method which is actually in use in most of the free countries. It does not as yet have a spectacular name, a great dialectical apparatus, a magniloquent philosophy, perfervid oratory, or mass emotion. But it is the method of those people who have had the largest experience in the art of self-government and the conduct of modern economic enterprise. That gives the method great authority, and the time has come, I believe, to recognize that there has appeared, principally among the English-speaking peoples, a method of social control which is not laissez-faire, which is not communism, which is not fascism, but the product of their own experience and their own genius.

I shall call it the method of free collectivism. It is collectivist because it acknowledges the obligation of the state for the standard of life and the operation of the economic order *as a whole*. It is free because it preserves within very wide limits the liberty of private transactions. Its object is not to direct individual enterprise and choice according to an official plan but to put them and keep them in a working equilibrium. Its method is to redress the balance of private actions by compensating public actions.

The system of free collectivism originates not in military necessity but in an effort to correct the abuses and overcome the disorders of capitalism. In the first instance it takes the form of measures which set limits within which private initiative is confined and fix standards to which it must conform. This part of the system has a long history and is well understood. It is based upon a recognition of the fact that initiative may be evil as well as good, and that it is the duty of the state to encourage initiative when it is socially beneficent and to discourage it when it is not.

Thus it comprises measures to prevent fraud as between buyers and sellers: honest weights and measures, the enforcement of equitable contracts, the suppression of counterfeiting and the misrepresentation of goods. It comprises measures to equalize the bargaining power of the consumer and of the employee: the regulation of public utilities, factory laws, and minimum wage laws. It comprises measures to break up monopolies, to discourage harmful enterprises, to prevent nuisances, to restrict speculation, to repress a too rampant individualism in the use of property. It comprises measures to insure the weak against the hazards of existence and to restrain the strong from accumulating excessive wealth and power.

The body of laws which regulates enterprise is enormous, and however foolish or unworkable some of these laws may be, no one imagines that all these laws are unnecessary. In fact, there is every reason to think that if a regime of free transactions is to be preserved, even more searching and comprehensive standards will have to be set for it. It is more than likely, for example, that secrecy in corporate accounting will have to be abolished, that all large enterprises will have to submit to publicly instituted systems of bookkeeping, and that their whole financial structure will become as visible as that of a railroad or a municipal corporation. For it is only by making publicly available to everyone the whole position of these enterprises that the relations of capital and labor, of corporation and investor, of industry and consumer can be lifted to a plane where transactions are really free because all the relevant facts are known. To preserve the reality of free contract it will almost surely be necessary to abolish the sham freedom of corporate secrecy.

But all of this does not go to the heart of the matter. It can prevent abuses. It does not reach the vital defect of individualism which is that the multitude of individual decisions is not sufficiently enlightened to keep the economy *as a whole* in working order. Regulation is essentially negative. In the main it merely forbids this or that. But it is not possible to prohibit by laws the cumulative errors which produce the cycles of boom and depression. The state cannot make laws against the excessive optimism of prosperity or the panic pessimism of the ensuing crash. Yet it is in this cycle that the supreme danger arises. For the social order has now become so intricate that any serious breakdown in its economy will unloose forces that may destroy it.

Not only is it impossible to control the rhythm of capitalism by regulating laws but the very attempt to do it is as likely as not to accentuate the violence of the maladjustment. The experience of

the post-war years has shown with great conclu-
siveness that the effort to control depression at
some particular point, say at the price of wheat, or
at the price of gold, or at the wage rate in some
sheltered industry, or at a threatened bank or railroad—merely makes a part of the economy rigid
and forces the rest of it to bend all the more.

The post-war economic cycle demonstrated
clearly that individual decisions were not sufficient
to create a lasting prosperity and that individuals
could not endure the remedy of individual readjustment. The classical theorists over-estimated
the enlightenment which is based on self-interest
and the fortitude based upon self-reliance. The
event has shown that the individual judgment upon
which they relied exclusively has in the crucial
cases meant that the individual followed the crowd.
Imitation, the herd instinct, the contagion of numbers, fashions, moods, rather than a truly enlightened self-interest, have tended to govern the
economy.

This submerging of individualism in mass behavior is the consequence of the increasing complexity of the economic order. The data for a
"sound" judgment are not any longer available to
most men. For an integral part of every judgment
is now a speculation on what other speculators will

do. Take, for example, a banker who makes a loan to a reliable individual for a useful project on ample security at existing values. By every conventional rule it is a sound loan. Yet it may be a bad loan for no other reason than that too many bankers have made too many equally sound loans to too many reliable individuals for too many similar projects. The algebraic sum of a great number of reputable transactions may easily prove to be a disaster for all. We have seen this illustrated again and again in recent years. We have seen it in another phase of the cycle, when the individual decision to call a loan and make himself liquid becomes a collective disaster if the whole mass of individuals is stricken with prudence at the same time.

It follows that if individuals are to continue to decide when they will buy and sell, spend and save, borrow and lend, expand and contract their enterprises, some kind of compensatory mechanism to redress their liability to error must be set up by public authority. It has become necessary to create collective power, to mobilize collective resources, and to work out technical procedures by means of which the modern state can balance, equalize, neutralize, offset, correct the private judgments of masses of individuals. This is what I mean by a

Compensated Economy and the method of Free Collectivism.

It is a conception which is not spun out of abstract theory. It is rather an induction from many experiments actually undertaken. The oldest example of the method is to be found in the operation of a highly developed central bank. The function of such a bank is to correct the decisions of the member banks. It is supposed to contract credit when they show a tendency to over-expand credit, and to make credit abundant when they are making it scarce. In the Nineteenth Century it was believed that a central bank was performing its compensatory function adequately when it managed the flow of domestic credit in such a way as to preserve the parity of the foreign exchanges without large shipments of gold. More recently central bankers have been called upon to manage the flow of domestic credit with a view to stabilizing domestic trade, and, since the war, but more especially since 1931, the maintenance of exchange parity has tended to become a secondary concern as compared with the internal equilibrium.

For the purposes of this discussion the different theories as to the objectives of central banking policy are of no consequence. The immediate point is that a public institution already exists of which the function is to compensate and balance private transactions at a vital point in the social economy. As that function becomes more clearly recognized, the procedure and the instruments needed to perform it more effectively can be invented and tested in practice. Experience has seemed to indicate, for example, that a central bank is a more powerful engine for controlling a boom than for overcoming a depression. Up to the present time the instruments of compensation available to a central bank have been chiefly the discount rate and the purchase and sale of securities in the open market. It appears that at least in the early stages of a boom it is possible to stop over-expansion of private credit by raising the rate and by selling securities. If the central bank could be relied upon to apply these remedies promptly and thoroughly, it might be that the situation would never get out of hand.

But we cannot afford to count upon it alone. We must be prepared for greater emergencies. When a severe depression sets in, the instruments of compensation now available to central banks are not very effective. Lowering the rate, making money cheap, and large open market purchases of securities, which put the banks in a position where theoretically they can expand credit, are not effective enough. They may work in the long run. But the long run is too long. Consequently experiments have been made, and others considered, to test new instruments of monetary management that have a more direct impact upon the general price level. These are the experiments with a variable price for gold and silver and with a managed supply of incontrovertible paper money. They concern us here only because they indicate the possibilities of far-reaching developments in the art of collective compensation of private transactions.

But it is not only through the central banks that the modern state can assert compensatory control. It can act directly upon the various markets. This method is also recognized and has been tested experimentally. The state is itself a great employer, a great consumer, a great investor, and a great borrower. It can in theory,—and with experience it can probably learn how actually to do this,— time its operations so as to offset and balance the actions of private employers, consumers, investors, and borrowers. This involves the long range planning of public works of all kinds, and action in accordance with those plans as circumstances require. These are immense difficulties, I know, but they are, I believe, the difficulties of inexperience with a new social mechanism. There is nothing inherently impossible about a policy which would require the government to raise taxes and reduce its debts in good times and to lower taxes and borrow in bad times, to curtail public works, which means its demand for labor and materials, when private employment is full, and to promote public works when private work is slack.

The compensatory form of collective control can be carried further into the domestic economy. The state now possesses instrumentalities which can produce most powerful effects. One of these is taxation. Through taxation it is possible to do many things besides raise revenue; indeed all taxes do have far-reaching social and economic consequences. Taxes can be raised so as to discourage all enterprise or any particular enterprise. They can be lowered in order to encourage all or any particular enterprise. They can be used to curtail consumption or capital investment. They can be used to encourage them. An ideal system of taxation would, therefore, be flexible so that rates rose when business was tending toward a boom and fell when it was slowing down. It would also be discriminating so as to encourage or discourage saving with a view to preserving the equilibrium between saving and investment.

Another powerful instrument is the state's control over the rates charged by common carriers and public utilities. These rates ought to rise in the upward phase of the business cycle and to fall in the downward phase, and under a proper system of reserves there is no inherent reason why public utilities should not be managed as a compensatory mechanism. It is even conceivable that they should be treated like public works, that they should make long-term plans of development, and that they should withhold projects in good times and push them in bad times. Thus, instead of competing for labor and materials with the rest of industry, they would complement the operations of private industry.

Such mechanisms, in conjunction with a strong central bank which was clear about its function, would provide an enormously powerful system of compensatory control. But they would still not be sufficient to keep the economy in balance. For no modern economy is self-contained, and it is, therefore, necessary to take measures to keep it in balance with the outer world. For that reason, modern nations will come, I should guess, to what amounts to a budgeting of their international payments. The state will be concerned not only with its own domestic budget but with the balance of payments across the national boundaries. It will seek to regulate those payments through a manipulation of tariffs, bounties, and through public control of the volume and at least the general direction of foreign investments. If the international budget shows a tendency to excessive imports, it may raise the barriers; if there is a tendency to excessive exports, it may lower the barriers. If the volume of foreign loans appears to be abnormally large, it will cause the investment houses to curtail them. If the loans are abnormally small, and the export trades are suffering in consequence, it will through guaranties or direct public financing expand foreign credits. These are, of course, details suggested to illustrate the point, which is that in a modern economy tariffs and foreign credits can and should be treated as instruments for keeping the budget of international payments in approximate balance. For only by doing this can private judgment be made to operate within reasonably safe limits.

I hope I have given enough concrete illustrations to demonstrate that a system of free collectivism, operating through a method of compensatory control, need not lack the means for powerful intervention in the operation of the capitalist order. Some of the difficulties of such a system I shall attempt to discuss later. For the moment I should like to dwell upon certain of its general characteristics which, in my opinion, make it not only a feasible but an attractive alternative to a directed economy and a regime of absolute collectivism.

3. THE TWO SYSTEMS COMPARED

To anyone steeped in the tradition of laissez-faire there may at first appear to be little difference between a directed economy and a compensated economy. Both call for the exercise of vast powers by the state, for continual and deep intervention in the economic order. Both are collectivist in that both rest on a recognition that the standard of life and the management of the economy as a whole are a collective responsibility and not solely an individual one.

Yet between the two conceptions there is a radical difference. Under absolute collectivism, be it of the fascist or communist type, the government is in fact the master, the citizen a subject and a servant. Under free collectivism, the government in its economic activities is in effect a gigantic public corporation which stands ready to throw its weight into the scales wherever and whenever it is necessary to redress the balance of private transactions. The initiative, throughout the whole realm of production and consumption, excepting only public utilities and public works reserved as instruments of compensatory control, remains in individual hands.

This initiative is subjected not to an official plan and to administrative orders, but to the play of prices representing the judgments and preferences of producers, consumers, and investors. Within extremely wide limits enterprise is free. Men decide for themselves, guided chiefly by their estimates of the profits they may obtain, what they will produce; guided chiefly by the opportunities available and their own aptitudes, they decide at what they will work; guided by their needs and tastes in relation to their incomes, they decide what they will consume and how much they will save.

These choices are not made for them by officials exercising the power of the state. Thus economic progress is determined by technological advance, by private enterprise, and by what might be described as the perpetual plebiscite of the markets. The object of the state's intervention is not to supplant this system but to preserve it by remedying its abuses and correcting its errors. The intervention takes the form not of commands and prohibitions but of compensatory measures.

The purpose of the intervention is not to impose

an official pattern upon all enterprise, but to maintain a working, moving equilibrium in the complex of private transactions. In substance, the state undertakes to counteract the mass errors of the individualist crowd by doing the opposite of what the crowd is doing; it saves when the crowd is spending too much; it borrows when the crowd is saving too much; it economizes when the crowd is extravagant, and it spends when the crowd is afraid to spend; it contracts when the crowd is expansive; it becomes enterprising when the crowd is depressed; it buys in sellers' markets and sells in buyers' markets; it taxes when the crowd is borrowing, and borrows when the crowd is hoarding; it becomes an employer when there is private unemployment, and it shuts down when there is work for all. Its ideal is to prevent excess; its general principle is not to impose a social order conceived by officials but to maintain in a changing order, worked out by the initiative and energy of individuals, a golden mean.

In the practice of statesmanship the compensatory method is, I believe, an epoch-making invention. For generations it has been supposed that an exclusive choice had to be made between collectivism and the freedom of private initiative, that the management of affairs had either to be

left to individuals or assumed by the state. Which-
ever way one looked at these alternatives, the prospect was unsatisfactory. To concentrate initiative
in officials was a certain way to kill initiative and
liberty and to establish a state which in the ordinary course of events was bound to be despotic
and inefficient. On the other hand, to let individualism run loose in a complex social order was to
let it run wild and thus to produce disorder and
injustice.

This dilemma is being resolved not by the argu-
ments of collectivists and individualists but by
the gradual uncovering of a new social principle.
It provides both for individual initiative and collective initiative. The one is not the substitute for
the other. The two are complementary. It is the
method of freedom. The authority of the government is used to assist men in maintaining the security of an ordered life. The state, though it is powerful, is not the master of the people, but remains,
as it must where they have liberty, their servant.

4. PLANNING IN AN ECONOMY OF ABUNDANCE

In making these comparisons and distinctions we
must of course remember that no principle of social organization is ever anywhere automatic and

all inclusive. When we speak of the feudal principle, or of laissez-faire capitalism, or of the fascist state, or of the planned economy of communism, we mean that a certain social principle is predominant in that society, that it describes the main relationship among men, that it is the criterion by which most judgments are arrived at.

In actual practice all social orders are a mixture of many theoretically inconsistent principles, some of them residues of the past, some perhaps embryonic of the future, some the inevitable exceptions to any rule which is applied to anything so complicated with variable elements as a human society. It is easy enough, therefore, for historians to discover remnants of the Roman system and anticipations of the capitalist method in the feudal age; it is easy to find traces of feudalism even in advanced capitalist societies, and under any form of collectivism there will be some freedom of individual enterprise. Yet, even though it is sometimes difficult to say whether a particular organism is a plant or an animal, we do not refuse to differentiate the two kingdoms because their frontiers are not absolutely precise, and we cannot

"... distinguish and divide
A hair 'twixt South and South West side."

So it is in these general conceptions with which we are dealing. When I suggest that absolute collectivism means decisions centralized in the state, I do not mean that every decision is centralized in the state. When I suggest that a free collectivism would compensate rather than command, redress the balance of private enterprises rather than administer them, I do not mean that it will not be found issuing commands and vetoes or administering many enterprises. I mean that the main prejudice, the predominant character in the one is official decision and in the other, private judgment. And the distinction, in spite of endless borderline cases which would be hard to classify is, I believe, a practical distinction of the utmost importance.

The fact that the capitalist economy is the product of private enterprise creates a strong presumption in favor of any principle which preserves private enterprise. It is significant that the planned economy of Russia has been established in a country where, contrary to the prophecies of Karl Marx, capitalism had had no considerable development. It is significant, too, that the corporative state of the fascists has been instituted in a country which, of all the western powers, had the least elaborate capitalist organization. It is, of course, relatively easy to supplant a system which is not deeply established. In fact, when the system has no strong roots and has had no great development, it may become necessary to operate it. But in America and in England the situation is very different. There the capitalist order has produced great results. It has distributed them among large masses of people who are attached to them. The vested interests which sustain the systems are not confined to the conspicuously rich; they are anchored in a very wide distribution of property and in the careers of multitudes, and it would be necessary to ruin millions before this attachment to the capitalist order was really broken. Not until something like that had occurred in Germany, a greater part of the nation having become hopelessly proletarian, did Germany, which has an advanced type of capitalist organization, fall into absolute collectivism.

In a country like the United States private initiative is so deep a habit that only a complete paralysis of the economy can even temporarily induce the people to submit to centralized regimentation. Almost the first thing the people recover, when business picks up even a little, is their resentment against dictation and their noble capacity as free men to growl when officialdom is too officious. To impose a planned economy upon a people with habits like these would be an undertaking so formidable that we may call it impossible.

But even if the people could be made docile to regimentation, the sheer complexity of the industrial system they have created would baffle any set of official planners who set out to direct it. Indeed, it can be shown, I believe, that the more varied are the products of an industrial order the less possible it becomes to deal with it as a planned economy. Let us suppose, to take a fantastic example, that the only food required and desired by men could be manufactured by applying the energy of the sun's rays to salt water. We could then stabilize production by balancing supply and demand with almost absolute accuracy: we could count the population, determine the number of calories needed, and make them. But suppose then that another food is invented, made, let us say, by fixing the nitrogen in the air. Men can now choose between two diets. Some prefer one. Some the other. Some a mixture of the two in varying proportions. It is not so easy now to stabilize production in the food industry. The supply cannot now be planned so accurately to meet the demand. For the demand is variable and the planners are now engaged in forecasting the future preferences rather than in supplying the absolute needs of the consumers.

As you add to the number of choices, you diminish your own power to forecast them, and by that token your power to plan production.

That is why institutions which desire to stabilize their operations and to operate according to a plan —armies, for example, and prisons, hospitals, and boarding houses, serve their meals table d'hôte and not à la carte. The principle has general validity: the opportunity to plan is in proportion to the limitation of the consumer's choice. It is easier to plan in prisons than in hotels, in the commissariat of an army than in a department store. It is easier to plan and stabilize men's uniforms than women's evening gowns, men's hats than women's hats, telephones than newspapers, school text books than new novels, garbage collection than modernist paintings. When Mr. Ford made the only satisfactory cheap car on the market, he could plan much more effectively than he can now that there are several cars in his class. And when he had the market to himself, he never changed his model and he always painted it black; now he changes his model and paints it all sorts of colors. Inevitably he is planning less and guessing more.

The consumer's choice may be limited either from the point of view of supply or of demand. There may be an inadequate supply of a necessary article. Or there may be an inadequate income, allowing only the purchase of necessary articles. Then planning is indispensable and relatively easy. Now, it is an interesting circumstance that all the actual experiments which can be cited by the enthusiasts of planning have been carried on where supply was insufficient. The two great examples are, of course, the war economy among the western nations and the Russian system.[1] During the war there was a shortage of almost all necessities, and planning consisted in rationing the inadequate supply to the more or less clearly defined needs of the army and the civilians. In Russia, too, there has never been anything but a shortage of everything, including skilled labor, and planning is the rational method of dealing with a shortage.

In fact, we are entitled to conclude, I think, that a planned economy is an economy of scarcity and works effectively only in a sellers' market. This truth has become very much more evident as a result of innumerable attempts in recent years to deal with the problem of glut, of over-supply, by the method of centralized planning. It has proved to be infinitely more difficult to plan a limitation of production in America than to plan an increase

[1] *Cf.*, e.g., George Soule's *A Planned Society*, Ch. VII and VIII.

of production in Russia. Is that because the Russians are better organizers than the Americans? Obviously not. Is it because they have communist principles and we have capitalist principles, because they are free of the profit motive and we are moved by it? That might be said until one realizes that the Russians in order to promote their plans for increasing production have been reintroducing the incentive of profit in the form of piece rates, wage differentials, and bonuses. So it cannot be maintained that Russian planning works better than American because the incentives are less selfish and more social. The real reason, I believe, is not psychological but economic. It is that under conditions of plenty, that is to say in markets where the buyer is master and has many choices, the producer is not in a position to plan because he is not in control of the situation. He may plan the supply of wheat, and if he raises the price, the consumer will turn to rye or corn. He attempts to stabilize silk; the consumer turns to rayon or cotton or wool. He attempts to stabilize railroad rates; people ride in busses or stay at home and play the radio.

The ideal of planning has yet to come to terms with an economy of abundance. Once a population has learned to produce large wealth over and above the level of mere subsistence, a competition arises not merely among the producers in an industry but among industries. Shall I buy a camera or a radio, a new car or a set of false teeth, gin and bitters or another hat, ice cream or a ticket to the movies, a tiled bathroom or a vacation at the seashore? These options can exist only in an economy of plenty. They do not exist seriously for the quartermaster-general of an army or for a War Industries Board or for the Gosplan in Russia. But they would baffle to the point of absolute confusion anyone who undertook to deal through a centralized plan with the American economy as an integrated enterprise.

The existence of plenty is a condition of liberty and multiplies the individual choices. These choices dominate production, render it speculative and unpredictable, and therefore intractable to planning. In an economy of plenty the consumer is master of the situation. The fundamental premise of a planned economy is that the producer is master of the market. When the consumer is master, as he is wherever there is ample production, it is the plebiscite of the markets,—the consumers picking and choosing according to their tastes—which will perform the function that in an economy of scarcity may be performed by centralized planning.

5. THE COMPENSATORY METHOD DURING
THE CRISIS

For these reasons I venture to believe with great confidence that modern capitalism of a highly developed sort cannot be brought under collective control by the method of regimentation and centralized decision. Since, however, collective control is necessary, it must of necessity, I believe, take the form of compensatory actions. This form of control is compatible with the variability, the complexity, and the dynamic character of the capitalist order. The strongest presumption in favor of it is that important examples of this method have been developed within the orbit of the capitalist system itself.

Central banking, when it is expert and self-conscious, the management of government budgets in progressive societies, the regulation of the international payments, are not only examples of the compensatory method in practice but auguries of its extension and development. They have the great virtue that when they are well administered, they do in fact exercise a controlling influence upon the rhythm of production and consumption, saving and investment.

It could be shown, I believe, with reasonable certainty that among the measures adopted by western governments to overcome the depression of 1929, only those measures have had a discernible influence in promoting recovery which are of the compensatory type. The British Government has used almost no measures except ones of this type, that is to say, inflationary monetary and credit policies, expenditures for relief and public works, and the regulation of the balance of international payments. We have employed similar measures. But parallel with them we have experimented with planning through regimentation. It is perhaps too early to say that the A.A.A. and the N.R.A. have failed to produce results commensurate with the effort exerted, but it is hardly open to dispute that it has been the compensatory measures, the management of the dollar and the inflationary expenditures through many channels, to the unemployed, to farmers, to depositors, and to debtors, which have had the most substantial and immediate effect in reviving trade and production. When one goes further into the matter, it is a coincidence so striking that perhaps it is more than a coincidence that our recovery in the spring of 1934, with N.R.A. and A.A.A., is no greater than the British, the Canadian, and Australian, without them; that, on the other hand, virtually all nations which have resorted to compensatory policies show much more definite signs of recovery than do those, like France and Holland and Switzerland, which have rejected them.

I do not wish to press the generalization too far. For obviously it is impressionistic, and we may live to learn many things we do not dream of now. But we have gone far enough, and have been passing through a sufficiently severe test, to warrant the conclusion that the method of compensatory action is as promising a way of dealing with the realities of the capitalist economy as any which has been tried or is now known. That this type of control has proved to be consistent with the working of the capitalist order in many countries and has given evidence of being able to influence it beneficially in the period of its profoundest disturbance, is ground for confidence that we are on the track of a social discovery which has great promise.

PART THREE

GOVERNMENT IN A REGIME
OF LIBERTY

OUR most serious doubts as to whether a free collectivism can be operated must arise when we contemplate the existing practice of political democracy. I do not mean to underestimate the technical difficulties of using compensatory measures to correct the working of private enterprise. They are very great.

For many problems of the first importance we do not have clear solutions. We do not know, for example, to what degree the stability of the general average of internal prices is a desirable objective, to what degree it is desirable to sacrifice the rigidity of the foreign exchanges to the stability of domestic purchasing power; it is not clear how far flexibility of wage rates, particular prices, and the costs represented by fixed charges, should or can be attained. There are, too, great administrative difficulties in a policy which calls for the long range planning of public works and the timing of their execution. But problems of this sort would be, it seems to me, not insoluble in a society where the preponderant opinion was in favor of the system and interested in their solution. They could be solved by men who wished to solve them. They are difficult now, not because they are in principle insoluble, but because we lack experience and have not yet the will to deal seriously with them.

Technical and administrative questions that are fully as difficult have arisen in every social order and would arise in any that can be conceived. It is not necessary, therefore, to prove that free collectivism possesses a ready-made solution of all its problems in order to justify it as a working principle. It is sufficient to show that it is compatible with the main characteristics of the economic order, that it is not antipathetic to its essential elements, that it is not a proposal to put square pegs in round holes or to mix oil with water. To claim more for it than that it is a viable method, which could, so to speak, live in the particular climate of modern industrialism, would be uncandid and unprofitable. Those who claim more for any new social concept are either self-deluded or they are more interested in persuasion than in finding the truth.

I. TRANSIENT MAJORITIES AND PRESSURE GROUPS

But the difficulties which arise from the side of political democracy, as it now operates in the United States for example, are formidable because they arise from a deep conflict of principle. Under popular rule the assumption is that the government should be governed by popular opinion. But the compensatory method of control, as we have seen, requires that the state shall act, almost continually, contrary to the prevailing opinion in the economic world. The question that arises immediately is how and whether the people will consent to a policy which calls for decisive actions which are in their longer interest but contrary to their immediate opinions. Will a democracy authorize the government, which is its creature, to do the very opposite of what the majority at any time most wishes to do?

The general problem is, of course, not a new one. The authors of the Constitution were acutely aware of it and in setting up the frame of government they provided checks and balances which would, as they put it, "refine the will" of the people. They had no illusions as to how pure democracy, that is to say government which is immediately responsible to transient majorities, would work. They knew that it meant the sacrifice of the long view to the short view, of the general interest to particular interests, of liberty to mass opinion, and of order to the turbulence of crowds. They foresaw clearly all the real difficulties of political democracy, and the Constitution is undoubtedly the greatest attempt ever made consciously by men to render popular rule safe for the nation as a whole, the local community, and the individual. By a limitation of powers and by their separation the makers of the Constitution sought to protect the citizen himself and his state against the tyranny of numbers and the nation as a whole against its own unconsidered opinions. They intended to prevent temporary majorities from exercising immediate powers. They did this by defining the subjects on which the majority could legislate, and then by making it possible to legislate only when there was agreement among three distinct representatives of the popular will, the House, the Senate, and the President, all selected by differently organized constituencies and at different times.

For various reasons, however, there has been a progressive popularization of the government, that is to say, all its separate organs have become increasingly responsive to the same prevailing opinion. The result is a system of government which is highly sensitive to immediate opinion. In practice this means, of course, that it is highly sensitive to articulate, willful, and organized opinion among the voters in the constituencies. The prevailing opinion is not the opinion which the majority would hold if it understood the question and had made its decision. It is the opinion which is held by those who are most directly interested in a question, or think they are, and two determined voters of the same opinion are naturally more influential than ten undecided and only vaguely interested voters. Popular government has, therefore, become particularly responsive to pressure groups, to those who know what they want as against the amorphous majority who do not know.

A free collectivism using the compensatory method of control would, under existing democratic institutions, be subject to constant conflicting pressures from organized interests. There is no use disguising or minimizing the seriousness of this difficulty, and for my part, I am prepared to concede that free collectivism is as incompatible with political democracy in its present manifestations as are the planned economy of communism or the corporate state of fascism. Democracy which responds sensitively to prevailing opinion with that opinion articulated in pressure groups is incapable of operating any government successfully in war or in peace where the government is called upon to intervene deeply in the social order. A direct democracy of this sort must, as Macaulay pointed out seventy-five years ago, "sooner or later destroy liberty or civilization or both." [1] If allowed to run without restraint, it would destroy civilization because the apparent interest of temporary majorities cannot be depended upon to safeguard the permanent general interest. What articulate groups are interested in at the moment has no necessary relation to their real interest, and a social order, particularly a complex one in which actuating causes are hidden and the impact of the true consequences delayed, cannot conceivably be governed by the attractive, the plausible, the self-regarding whims and impulses of the moment. So certain is the devastation of absolute democracy that the people themselves will follow a dictator who offers to save them from their own misgovernment.

We must be prepared, I believe, to face the conclusion that it is not only capitalism but democ-

---

[1] *Letter to H. S. Randall, Mar. 23, 1857,* pub. by N. Y. Public Library, 1925.

racy that has to be reconstructed. If individualism with laissez-faire is unworkable and must give way to a form of collectivism in which the state is responsible for preserving a balance among private transactions, then absolute democracy is an unworkable way to organize political power. To discharge its new responsibility public authority has to be reasonably independent of transient opinion and organized pressure. Absolute democracy is as a matter of fact the political reflection of economic laissez-faire. The neutral and irresponsible state, having in ordinary times no vital functions to perform, could be responsive to irresponsible opinion. But as the state becomes charged with collective duties implicating all the permanent interests of the nation, it must of necessity equip itself for the task by divorcing itself from the pressure of unconsidered and temporary opinions. Absolute democracy was tolerable when the state was neutral. It was tolerable because normally it operated on the circumference and not upon the center of the economy. It could be foolish or corrupt and no great harm was done as long as it could not or did not intervene at the heart of the enterprises by which men live. But when the state becomes active, the ways of democracy have either to be adapted to the new responsibilities, or democracy itself will be overthrown.

2. REPRESENTATIVE DEMOCRACY: THE RETURN TO ITS FIRST PRINCIPLES

We can best arrive at an understanding of the way in which democracy will have to be reformed by reconsidering the task which the state would have to perform in a compensated economy. It would have, in brief, to manage credit, its own budget, and the budget of international payments. The purpose of this management would be to redress the balance of the mass of private transactions. Since this would require a continual contrariness to the popular mood, the managers of the compensatory devices would have to be independent of the currents of contemporary politics. They would have to enjoy an independence roughly comparable with that of the federal judiciary and of healthy central banks.

If we ask ourselves, then, what is the principal reason why a modern democratic state cannot now be trusted to administer policies that require independence and foresight, devotion to the general interest rather than to local or special interests, to the long result rather than the immediately apparent, we shall find it, I believe, in the fact that legislatures have acquired the initiative in fiscal matters. They have arrogated to themselves the power to propose expenditures, taxes, and loans and to compel the executive to make the expenditures and collect the revenue. These are powers which a representative assembly, particularly one elected by territorial constituencies, cannot hope to exercise in the general interest and in the light of the larger consequences. On the other hand, an executive which has lost the initiative in fiscal matters is virtually impotent. As a result, no organ of government is able to take the long view or to represent the general interest.

When the assembly acquires and the executive loses the initiative in fiscal matters, the natural equilibrium of constitutional government is upset. This is the root of the perversion and corruption of representative democracy and of the weakness of democratic governments. It is the most certain cause of their ultimate destruction.

In the development of modern constitutional liberty we can see, as Professor McIlwain [1] has said, that it has come through the power of the purse and the principle that "supply and redress

[1] Charles Howard McIlwain, *The Growth of Political Thought in the West*, pp. 370 *et seq.*

of grievances go hand-in-hand." In the Middle
Ages, at the beginnings of our institutions, the accepted doctrine was that the king's authority was
absolute in its sphere but that its sphere did not
include the property of his subjects. It followed
from this that "redress must be bought: it cannot
be legally forced; and second, that supply must
be asked: it cannot be legally taken." When his
revenues from his own feudal estates became inadequate, the king had, therefore, to buy grants
of revenue with grants of political favors. In this
exchange the principle was evolved that the executive is responsible to the people, and it is in
this sense that the power of the purse is the crux
of constitutional liberty. In the American tradition
it is represented by the slogan: no taxation without
representation. A government which must go to
the people's representative for its funds must respect their wishes. It must make an accounting to
them.

Historically, then, the power of the purse has
meant the power of the assembly to refuse revenues and to grant them on terms. But in modern
times in many states the power of the purse has
been transformed into the right of the assembly
to initiate and direct expenditure. The representatives no longer tell the executive what he may

spend. They tell him what he must spend, not merely how much he may tax, but how much he must tax, not merely what he may borrow, but what he must borrow. This conversion of the power of the purse from consent to compulsion, from a negative to a positive principle, has produced the corruption, the waste, the injustice, the short-sightedness and the maladministration which are destroying popular faith in representative government, have paralyzed it in times of crisis, have made it necessary to suspend the normal working of representative institutions in all grave emergencies, and have wrecked them in many lands. By centering in the legislature powers which it cannot wisely exercise, by robbing the executive of powers he must have if he is to administer the state, the whole machinery of government is perverted, paralyzed and degraded.

In theory, of course, the elected legislator is supposed to be chosen by his constituency but to represent the nation. This is the doctrine advanced by Burke in his famous speeches to the electors of Bristol.[1] But as a matter of fact the tenure of the legislator depends upon the approval of a majority of his constituents. His own self-interest and theirs both impel him, therefore, to become their

[1] Robert H. Murray, *Edmund Burke*, p. 238.

delegate, their ambassador. Occasionally, a man of outstanding genius will arise and hold his office as a national statesman and be re-elected because his constituents are proud of him. He is, however, the exception. The mechanism of representation exerts a constant mighty pressure to make the politician the servant of the voters who elect him. When, therefore, he goes to the capital city and has the power to initiate expenditures, to propose pensions, public works, subsidies, doles, grants-in-aid, and tariffs, his constituents at home will expect him to exercise his initiative. They will divide into self-regarding groups who look to him to do business for them. A collection of these self-regarding groups becomes the dominant majority in his constituency. To satisfy them the representative must make bargains with other representatives so that together they may make up a majority in the assembly capable of passing the laws which produce the grants and the privileges which are the price of re-election set by the constituents.

It is idle to pretend that a modern state can be wisely governed by coalitions of delegates responding to local coalitions of self-regarding pressure groups. It would be absurd to suppose that a state subject to such control could administer a planned economy or a free collectivism. The system is set up in such a way as to put a premium upon particular interests as against the general interest. The electorate becomes habituated to think of its representatives as men sent to the capital to get things for them. Those who get them are debauched. Those who do not become cynical or disheartened. The politicians, compelled to buy their re-election with public money tend to become under the law of the survival of the fittest the kind of men who like to do that and have no other idea of the public service. There is much too little room in such a system for scrupulous and public-spirited men.

In time of national crisis the weaknesses of the system are disclosed. When it becomes really important to bring the national economy into balance, to act simply and decisively in the general interest, it transpires that the legislature and executive are trapped in a maze of entrenched privileges. Nobody has the power to govern. The executive is bound by commitments which the legislature has made; the legislature is bound by its own commitments. Representatives cannot vote to repeal the privileges which they have initiated except by risking their own political extinction. The executive cannot suspend those privileges except by obtaining the initiative which the legislature has

assumed. It is a hopeless deadlock which it is possible to resolve only by changing the balance of the
constitution in order to restore to the executive his
initiative in fiscal matters. It has been necessary to
do this in all countries in recent years. In some it
has been done by overthrowing the democratic
state; in some by suspending the powers of the
parliament and governing by decree; in others, by
a pressure of public opinion and party discipline
which have given the executive "leadership" for
the period of the emergency.

But whatever the method of meeting the situation, the remedy in all cases is in principle the
same; the initiative is transferred from territorial
delegates who represent local and special interests
to the executive who in theory represents the
whole nation. This is a political revolution which
is temporarily necessary in any grave crisis and is
permanently necessary if the modern state is to
discharge the great task of regulating the national
economy.

It becomes a revolution which imperils constitutional liberty if the legislature loses not merely its
right to initiate but also its right to consent. Only
where the two powers are in balance,—the executive proposing, the representative assembly con-
senting or rejecting,—is political liberty soundly

organized. Where the balance is destroyed, the assembly having usurped the initiative, the corruption and weakness of the government will cause the pendulum to swing to a dictatorship in which the executive proposes and asks no one's consent. To restore to the executive the initiative in all matters requiring expenditures of funds and the raising of revenue is undoubtedly something of a political revolution in countries where the legislature has acquired the initiative. But it is a revolution which would conserve the vitality of representative government by returning to the historic principles from which it has evolved.

In Great Britain, where these principles originated and have been most jealously preserved, the Commons, as Sir Erskine May has put it, "do not vote money unless it be required by the Crown, nor impose or augment taxes unless the taxation be necessary for the public service, as declared by the Crown through its constitutional advisers." [1] Thus the government cannot raise money or spend it without the authority of Parliament. And Parliament cannot vote money or levy taxes except at the demand of the government. It is perhaps no

[1] Sir T. Erskine May, *Parliamentary Practice*. The passage quoted is taken from Sir Courtenay Ilbert's *Parliament, Its History, Constitution and Practice*, p. 90.

accident that in meeting the crisis of these past
years the British among all the peoples have had
to depart the least from the normal practices of
their constitution. For their political system is
more nearly in balance than any other. It is most
favorable, therefore, to a satisfactory combination
of executive independence with responsiveness to
public opinion. Among the British people representative institutions have developed according to
their original genius. The initiative has remained
with the executive; consent comes from the representative assembly.

Where this natural and necessary balance of
powers is upset, popular government works badly,
and in great crises, does not work at all.

3. PRESSURE GROUPS IN AN UNBALANCED
ECONOMY

If we look at our political system as it now operates, and try to imagine what would happen if
it were charged with the task of applying compensatory measures through a management of money
and of government expenditures and taxation, and
through the regulation of the balance of international payments, most men will conclude that
pressure groups would confuse and distort the

whole effort. I do not wish to minimize this difficulty by any kind of special pleading. It is the great problem of government and there is no short and easy solution. Yet if we admit that the problem is insoluble we are in a vicious circle. For in one form or another the state is compelled to intervene deeply in the economic order; if it cannot achieve sufficient independence from the pressure of special groups and of temporary opinions to govern in the general interest, it cannot meet the obligation which under modern conditions it cannot escape.

It is necessary, therefore, to look more closely at these pressure groups, particularly those whose demands bear upon the management of credit, expenditure and taxation. I leave out of account, as not directly pertinent to the problem, those groups which are interested in moral reforms or in questions not deeply involving the operation of the economy, as, for example, prohibition and temperance, pacifism and militarism, education and the administration of criminal justice.

Now what is it that causes producers, shippers, consumers, creditors, debtors, employers and employees to organize, to send lobbyists to Washington, and to put pressure upon the government? Is it not primarily the conviction that they must defend their interests as they understand them? Occasionally a group will organize for aggressive purposes, to obtain a special privilege; still oftener aggressive purposes will be subtly introduced into the agitation of a group which thinks it is acting defensively. But by and large a pressure group made up of a large number of citizens is convinced that it is fighting for its rights. It is threatened with the competition of foreign goods. It is paying too high rates for transportation or power. It is paying too high prices. It is receiving too low prices. It cannot meet its old debts. It cannot obtain new credit. It is being sweated in the competition of the labor market. It is being gouged by monopolists of labor, or big business, or finance. It is in distress and must be helped. It is suffering from too high taxes.

If we consider these varied and conflicting pressures, are we not forced to the conclusion that principally they originate in the instability of the economic order and are the public evidences of it? What are these people pressing for? They are pressing to correct their own position, to achieve for themselves that stability of sufficient income which the system of private enterprise does not automatically produce. Where the political system is set up so as to preserve executive initiative in fiscal matters, pressure groups are discouraged. They do not find it easy to act upon the government. Where the financial initiative is in the legislature, they are encouraged to exert pressure. Because it is so easy to make it successful, everyone presses. When everyone does it, everyone tends to feel that he has to do it. But while an improper distribution of political power greatly aggravates the pressure of groups, it is the fact that the economy is rarely in balance for any length of time which provokes these groups to action. In substance they are attempting to achieve by special measures the result which a compensated economy, if successfully administered, would achieve by its general measures.

Living in an economy where the pendulum of prices, wages, profits and opportunity swings erratically from one extreme to another, men organize to make themselves secure, to neutralize the effects, and to obtain relief. During the hard times of the past five years we have seen the phenomenon in all countries and among all classes of the population. The whole vast structure of tariffs, quotas, exchange controls, moratoria, bounties, guaranties, doles, of price fixing, the restriction of output and the regimentation of enterprise, has been erected bit by bit through the pressure of separate groups frantically trying to stabilize their own position in a radically unbalanced economic order. But what we have seen during this emergency is simply the magnification of the ordinary processes of democracy in a highly individualistic economy.

Thus it is that the general interest, viewed in the larger consequences, tends to be submerged under the demands of men seeking immediate protection and relief.

4. PROLETARIANISM

In studying this problem we must, however, be careful to see it in perspective. It would be easy to fall into the fallacy of supposing that it is necessary or desirable to stop all the pressures of special groups. That is impossible. As Mr. Charles Beard has said, "no scheme will eliminate diversity of interests" and "government inevitably reflects them." [1] A dictatorship may suppress some group interests; it will certainly be powerfully influenced by others. To imagine that a nation might be composed of individuals who are devoted only to the abstract general good is a Utopian fantasy. In the ordinary processes of the best government that it is

[1] Charles A. and William Beard, *The American Leviathan*, p. 219.

possible to conceive, public officials would still have to accommodate policy to the conflict of diverse interests. The real problem is not how to abolish these interests or how to silence them. It is how to keep them manageable, how to prevent them from becoming intransigent and irresistible. If that can be done, the diverse groups will tend to check each other, and it is then not impossible to frame policies which compromise their demands and reconcile their claims.

The situation really tends to become unmanageable when in the electorate there is a considerable body of voters who have nothing to lose. They are the reserves from which are recruited political machines and political armies. To their demands there are no countervailing considerations. They do not have a sufficient stake in the social order as a whole, and, being outside the circle of established rights, they cannot and do not count the costs. When they are organized, they form a compact minority in the state which is stronger than the disorganized majority. If a pressure group can attach itself to such a political machine, it can then exert a pressure which is far greater than its real strength, and its demands will tend to prevail as against those of opposing groups which do not have the backing of the dominant party.

Let us take as an illustration the Tammany system, not because it is exceptionally bad but because it is broadly typical of popular government in which general and long-term interests are sacrificed to special and immediate interests. Reformers attack Tammany on two grounds. They cry out that it serves the Interests. They cry out that it panders to the People. They call it an engine of plutocracy and they say it is organized demagogy. Both charges are substantially true. To perpetuate itself in office Tammany makes as large a number of voters as possible dependent upon the public treasury. It is not necessary that they should be a numerical majority. It is sufficient to collect a compact minority who live on public money; it will normally prevail over the amorphous majority who are divided in their allegiance and vague or indifferent as to what they want. The compact minority of jobholders and direct beneficiaries, together with their dependents and friends, normally constitute a solid and dependable basis of political power. This power is then used, in the first instance, of course, to satisfy this compact minority. The machine will protect its supporters, that is to say, it will protect itself, against all other interests. But if it is securely entrenched with its own adherents, it is open and ready to do business with public utilities, landlords, contractors, and any other organized interest. It deals in franchises, public improvements, real estate values, exemptions, privileges, monopolies. To do business with it is usually profitable. It is convenient. Not to do business with it is troublesome and often hazardous. Thus the enterprising class in the city tends to make terms with the machine, sometimes to obtain a profit, more frequently perhaps to avoid loss, delay, and obstruction.

This system was not invented by Tammany. Nor is it confined to Tammany. A similar system, though with different groups and different interests, prevailed in the Republican Party during its long period of dominance in the national government. On the side of the electorate it had the pension system, the public lands, the federal patronage, and the porkbarrel; on the side of the so-called interests it had the tariff, the natural resources of the public domain, and subsidies. The party had principles and ideals, no doubt. But its political organization was held together by these payments and privileges. The notion, so generally held by reformers, that a ruling party is a mere creature of the so-called interests is a half-truth which misrepresents the reality. The interests would not be strong enough to control the government in the face of a democratic electorate unless the electorate itself has been divided into an amorphous mass of vague or habitual voters and a compact minority of self-regarding voters. The political machine is the broker among the interested groups, the organizer and reconciler of their demands.

When representative government is perverted, we are likely to find that political power is wielded by organizations recruited from the two ends of the social scale: from the proletariat and the plutocracy. I use these terms for the sake of brevity and convenience. It is not necessary for the purposes of this argument to enter the mazes of the dialectical debate which must follow the attempt to define them precisely. By the proletariat I mean those who do not have property or a dependable occupation which *assures* them an income for their principal needs. By the plutocracy I mean those who have more income than they need for their personal use and enjoyment. The characteristic of the proletarian is, from this point of view, not the meagerness of his income but its uncertainty. He lives in a condition of economic insecurity. Thus a small farmer who is able to obtain a living from his own land would not be a proletarian, however much he may lack the comforts of modern existence. Nor would a highly skilled artisan be a proletarian, though under abnormal conditions of prolonged unemployment he may become one. On the other hand, the characteristic of the plutocracy, as I see it, is the possession of wealth, which is not needed for personal consumption or as the working capital of personal enterprise and is, therefore, an instrument of power exercised generally for the accumulation of more wealth and more power.

It is from among those who are economically insecure that there are recruited the popular pressure groups to which politicians are most immediately responsive: the veterans demanding pensions, the unemployed demanding public jobs and doles, the office seekers looking for a place on the public payroll. It is from the plutocracy, as I have defined it, that there are drawn the seekers of government privileges and exemptions. Although in theory the proletariat and the plutocracy are in conflict, in fact they tend to combine in a dangerous union and to dominate the state. We can see the process under a magnifying glass in the fascist countries where the plutocracy finances the private army that the dictator recruits among the unemployed and the disinherited. But essentially the same union of the two extremes is achieved in most democratic nations through the medium of the dominant political party.

In the face of this union it is difficult to govern in the general interest and for the longer consequences.

5. THE MIDDLE CONDITION AND THE SECURITY OF THE STATE

We come then to the conclusion that it is not the pressure groups as such which make it impossible for the state to act in the general interest and for the long view, but pressure groups attached to and reinforced by political machines recruited from those who are intransigent because they have nothing to lose. It is by proletarian insecurity that free government is ruined. This is an old conclusion. It has been verified again and again throughout history, and proclaimed by political thinkers in all ages where men have sought to combine security with freedom.[1]

Aristotle stated it clearly when he said that:[2] "the best political community is formed by citizens of the middle class," and that

[1] *Cf.* Arthur N. Holcombe, *The New Party Politics.*
[2] *Politics,* Book IV, Chap. 11.

"those states are likely to be well administered, in which the middle class is large, and larger if possible than both the other classes, or at any rate than either singly; for the addition of the middle class turns the scale and prevents either of the extremes from being dominant . . . this is the class of citizens which is most secure in a state, for they do not, like the poor, covet their neighbors' goods; nor do others covet theirs, as the poor covet the goods of the rich; and as they neither plot against others nor are themselves plotted against, they pass through life safely . . . Great, then, is the good fortune of a state in which the citizens have a moderate and sufficient property; for where some possess much, and the others nothing, there may arise an extreme democracy or a pure oligarchy; or a tyranny may grow out of either extreme . . ."

With him we may well repeat the prayer of Phocylides:

"Many things are best in the mean; I desire to be of a middle condition in my city."

It is by the reduction of the extremes and the fostering and the maintenance of a middle condition among its people that a modern state can make itself most solid and most serviceable. When a large class are insecure and a powerful class possess extraordinary private influence, the incentives to

exploit the state for special purposes are too strong
to be resisted by the public spirit of the disinterested and the neutrality of the uninterested. In the
proletariat there is a reservoir of voters who, lacking a definite stake in the social order, are responsive to bribery and enchantment; in the plutocracy
there are men of exceptional enterprise and au-
dacity, who, as Aristotle said "have too much of
the goods of fortune, strength, wealth, friends, and
the like" and "are neither willing nor able to submit to authority." Therefore, to establish a state, of
which the government is representative, in a community which desires to preserve an economy run
by private transactions but held in balance by collective action, it is necessary to take as an avowed
object of policy the abolition both of the proletariat
and of the plutocracy.

In making this avowal we must not let ourselves be distracted or confused by the cry that
this is socialism, Marxism, the class war, and con-
fiscation. It is none of these things. It is their very
opposite. It is a policy which is frankly and un-
ashamedly middle class in its ideal; it envisages
a nation in which private property for private use
and private security is firmly established because
most men possess it; it is opposed to the condition
of proletarianism as a denial of the security, the

independence and the liberty which sufficient property will provide; it is opposed to plutocracy because the inordinate accumulation of property means an inordinate accumulation of power. This is not a project to abolish private property and to make all the people servants of the state. On the contrary, it is a project to make the mass of people independent of the state: that they may be free citizens, who need not be fed by the government, who have no impelling reason to exploit the government, who cannot be bribed, who cannot be coerced, who have no fear of the state and expect no favors. For their livelihood and personal security rest upon private property and vested rights, not upon the acts of officials.

6. PRIVATE PROPERTY AS THE FOUNDATION OF LIBERTY

It has been the fashion to speak of the conflict between human rights and property rights, and from this it has come to be widely believed that the cause of private property is tainted with evil and should not be espoused by rational and civilized men. In so far as these ideas refer to plutocratic property, to great impersonal corporate properties, they make sense. These are not in reality private properties. They are public properties privately controlled and they have either to be reduced to genuinely private properties or to be publicly controlled. But the issue between the giant corporation and the public should not be allowed to obscure the truth that the only dependable foundation of personal liberty is the personal economic security of private property.

The teaching of history is very certain on this point. It was in the mediæval doctrine that to kings belong authority but to private persons, property, that the way was discovered to limit the authority of the king and to promote the liberties of the subject. Private property was the original source of freedom. It is still its main bulwark. Recent experience confirms this truth. Where men have yielded without serious resistance to the tyranny of new dictators, it is because they have lacked property. They dared not resist because resistance meant destitution. The lack of a strong middle class in Russia, the impoverishment of the middle class in Italy, the ruin of the middle class in Germany, are the real reasons, much more than the ruthlessness of the Black Shirts, the Brown Shirts, and the Red Army, why the state has become absolute and individual liberty is suppressed. What maintains liberty in France, in Scandinavia, and in the English-speaking countries is more than any other thing the great mass of people who are independent because they have, as Aristotle said, "a moderate and sufficient property". They resist the absolute state. An official, a teacher, a scholar, a minister, a journalist, all those whose business it is to make articulate and to lead opinion will act the part of free men if they can resign or be discharged without subjecting their wives, their children, and themselves to misery and squalor.

For we must not expect to find in ordinary men the stuff of martyrs, and we must, therefore, secure their freedom by their normal motives. There is no surer way to give men the courage to be free than to insure them a competence upon which they can rely. Men cannot be made free by laws unless they are in fact free because no man can buy and no man can coerce them. That is why the Englishman's belief that his home is his castle and that the king cannot enter it, like the American's conviction that he must be able to look any man in the eye and tell him to go to hell, are the very essence of the free man's way of life.

This is the substance of liberty, not perhaps as dialecticians or doctrinaires might define it, but as the peoples who have won and maintained their liberties have learned to understand it.

7. THE RIGHT TO WORK

From this point of view the extinction of proletarian insecurity and the reduction of plutocratic
power are means to an end: which is to fortify the
regime of liberty upon a foundation of private
property. And here again, I must say in a paren-
thesis that it is not necessary or possible to attempt
too precise a definition of private property. I mean
by it substantial security of income necessary to existence. Whether that income is derived in whole
or in part from land, stocks, bonds, wages, salaries,
pensions, insurance, does not matter provided the
individual is assured that in the normal course of
events he can depend upon it. His income must
not be at the mercy of electoral majorities, official
decrees, administrative decisions, or the preferences
of employers and other superior persons. It must
be safe for a reasonably prudent man. It must not
require inside knowledge, speculative genius, or
exceptional business ability to preserve it. He must
feel that he is secure.

The question is how such a policy can most effectively be pursued. I believe that the effective
method is to attack proletarian insecurity. If my
analysis was correct when it purported to show that

the political power of the plutocracy was founded
upon the purchaseable votes of the disinherited,
then the cure is to strike at proletarianism, and ab-
sorb those who are now insecure into the middle
class, attaching them to it by their vested interest,
and multiplying its power by their numbers. If
that is done, the plutocratic power will fall, or at
least be reduced to a point where it can easily be
mastered. It will not be able to recruit armies of
the disinherited. The opposite method, which is to
strike at plutocracy first, to devise fetters to bind
it, to harry it and hamstring it, is at once destructive
and ineffective. It produces immense but inconclu-
sive conflicts, tends to paralyze the working of the
economic order, and almost invariably ends in a
sharp reaction. For a merely anti-plutocratic policy
is essentially vindictive and punitive; it does not
make the mass of people any more secure to make
the rich insecure; but it may and usually does in-
terrupt production and trade, and this produces a
discontent which is easily turned against the reformers. On the other hand, a policy which is
primarily anti-proletarian, which puts the chief
emphasis upon constructing property for the un-
propertied, is the radical method in that it goes to
the root of the matter. It relieves the proletariat of
its grievance and the plutocracy of its mercenaries,

and thus makes preponderant in the state those who are in the middle condition.

The principles of such a policy are indicated, I believe, by the answer to a simple question: when do proletariat and plutocracy appear in a society? They appear, do they not, when there is no more free land, when the existing resources have been pre-empted? The social disease of proletarianism is not serious where the frontier is still open, when the disinherited have the opportunity to migrate and stake out their own inheritance. It is not serious in a society where land and wealth are evenly distributed and the population is stable. It is serious where there are many who cannot establish themselves on properties of their own.

Broadly speaking, the possibilities open to the pioneer are now greatly restricted. The best lands are taken up. There are stringent laws against migration. The modern urban proletariat has become unfitted for the life of the pioneer. Much can be done to mitigate these conditions. An enlightened policy for the utilization of land and for the decentralization of industry would open up many new opportunities. It may be possible to do something through the reform of education to overcome the blank, helpless specialization of the deracinated city dweller. But the main problem will remain. It is necessary somehow to construct within the framework of our complicated machine civilization the moral equivalent of the opportunity to stake out private property in virgin territory.

The experimental beginnings of such a policy are to be found in the social services and the social insurance which all advanced industrial communities are compelled to provide. Through these social services, collective enterprise supplies education, health, housing and recreation to those who cannot buy them out of their own incomes. Through systems of insurance against accident, disease, old age, and unemployment; through pensions to the incapacitated and the handicapped some public provision is made for those who are without sufficient independent means. But all of these measures, though they are indispensable under modern conditions, are inadequate and, both to those who receive and to those who must pay for them, subtly repugnant. However much they may be disguised, they are and are felt to be an elaborate system of charity which draws a line between the free citizens and the dependent population. It is the ineradicable vice of this whole mass of palliative reforms that they create a caste of those who have to be specially taken care of and thus destroy the fellowship of morally equal men.

What they do is to provide substitutes for independence and relief for the insecure. They do not provide the opportunity to earn and acquire independence. In a modern state that can be done only, I believe, by recognizing the right to work as one of the rights of man. I know that it is not the fashion to speak of the rights of man, and I understand the theoretical and metaphysical objections to the doctrine of natural rights. All rights are, no doubt, ultimately a creation of the state and exist only where they are organized by the government.[1] There are, however, certain rights of the individual which, except in nations that are sunk in absolutism, are provided by the state. There are rights of personal liberty, rights of political participation, rights of property, rights of local self-government. To these rights we must add, I believe, the right of access to remunerative work.

The organization of this right requires the overcoming of technical, administrative, and financial difficulties. But there is no reason to think they are insuperable. The essential principle is to have on hand at all times varied projects of useful public work on which any citizen may find employment when he needs it. The possibilities of useful public

[1] *Cf.* John W. Burgess, *The Foundation of Political Science*, Ch. VIII.

work are really inexhaustible. There is no end to what can be done in any nation to conserve its natural resources and develop them, to drain and reclaim its swamps and its deserts, to reconstruct cities and rural districts for the sake of health, beauty, and convenience. The Citizens Conservation Corps and the Civil Works Administration, hastily improvised as they were, and open to many criticisms in the details of their administration, have demonstrated, I believe, that the policy is practicable and sound. It is not the poverty of the public treasury but poverty of the public imagination which creates the real difficulties here; that, and a misguided and over-sophisticated commercialism, which identifies all productive effort with the immediate price in the marketplace. I am no enemy of the price system as the main regulator of production. These lectures have been a defense of the essential principles of that system. But there is such a thing as working for future use rather than for present sales, and the public works I have in mind have this character. A nation cannot impoverish itself by employing its labor to improve its resources and its equipment. It is not production but idleness, —it is unused materials and unused men—that are in the long run intolerably expensive.

It is possible then to establish the right to work

by projecting public works and executing them so as to offset scarcity and glut in the market for private labor. The operating principle should clearly be to pay wages which represent an adequate minimum in the locality. By making them adequate for a bare but self-respecting existence, the oppression and sweating of labor is discouraged. The citizen has an alternative to accepting an intolerable wage bargain. By making them no more than adequate, he is provoked to look to private employment, or to go pioneering on his own initiative for a higher standard of life. The financing of such public works would fall within the domain of monetary and credit management; the decision as to whether to pay for them out of savings and taxes or by borrowing and inflation should depend upon whether the economic order in general required contraction or expansion to keep it in balance.

These are details, immensely important details, but details. It is the principle that matters. If we seek to go to the root of modern insecurity it is here—in the insecurity of those who have no vested right to a livelihood. They are the disinherited and their lot is pitiable. On the sheer ground of human decency, let alone of human brotherhood, we are called upon to relieve it. But if these considerations do not move us, then it is the menace of the insecure which we must appreciate in all its gravity and its far-reaching consequences. It is from them that are drawn the evil powers by which the state is corrupted, and it is only by a policy which renders them secure that the modern state can itself be secure.

The establishment of the right to work is consistent with the method of a compensated economy. It is inherent in the method since it calls for collective enterprises whenever private enterprise is slack. A free collectivism would seek to guarantee at all times the opportunity to labor.

8. CONCLUSION

The question which we started with was whether representative democracy could be reconciled with the principles of a compensated economy. The answer we have come to is that a compensated economy is itself most likely to mitigate the normal pressure of interested groups and that, in guaranteeing the right to work, it strikes at the root of political instability and at the conditions under which pressure groups become intransigent. I do not mean to argue that a resort to these principles will automatically make a nation public spirited,

disinterested, and intelligent. They are no substitutes for civic virtue, for a great tradition, for
loyalty to the state, and for devoted leadership. I
do, however, mean to argue that they provide a
method available to an enlightened people by
which it can correct those very conditions from
which spring the most dangerous abuses of democracy; and further, that in so far as a compensated
economy can be administered, its tendency will be
to make democracy work better.

Representative government, as it has developed
under laissez-faire in most countries, *is* incompatible with a state which accepts responsibility for the
economy as a whole. But the method of free collectivism goes to the base of those disorders which
most commonly make democracy irresponsible. By
this method political and economic liberty can, I
believe, be made secure. Is there any other? It is
impossible to go back to laissez-faire and the neutral state. And only through endless misery could
nations with a highly developed capitalism and old
democratic traditions be subjected to absolute collectivism and a planned economy. Therefore, until
some other method is put forward which meets the
conditions of the modern world, we may say that
free collectivism, as indicated in the policies of the
English-speaking countries during the present

crisis, is the method of liberty in the Twentieth Century as laissez-faire was its method in the Nineteenth.

The procedure is new. The ideal is old. It is the ideal of the free man secure as against all the principalities and powers of the world. Its permanent concern is for those who are, as Aristotle described them, in the middle condition. Its special concern is to bring as many as possible to this middle condition. Free men with vested rights in their own living: men like these alone, and not employees of the state or the disinherited who today walk the streets and are at home nowhere, can constitute a free society.

In their independence liberty has its roots down deep in human nature. In their hands the state is most nearly representative of the general good. With them peace and order are most likely to prevail against the violence of factions and the stratagems of adventurers. By them the public business is most likely to be coolly and prosaically conducted. For in the orbit of their own independence there is ample scope for initiative and adventure and excitement, and they need not seek it in the streets. They are too firmly established in their own separate interests to be easily susceptible to the contagious fevers of huddled and amorphous crowds. Let it be said that they are bourgeois and dull. They live and let live. Let it be said that they do not respond readily to a grandiose and magniloquent tempo in public affairs; that they count the costs and are not easily impressed, in fact that they rather dislike what is too clever and too original. They have hold of the substance of liberty and they cling to it. They are stubborn and careful. But they have self-respect and, of their fate, though it be a small one and private, they are the masters.

At the bar where the verdicts of history are rendered they need apologize to no one for the part which free men play in the advance of civilization. Their way of life rests upon the conviction that no man and no set of men are wise enough or good enough to determine the destinies of mankind. In each child that is born there are possibilities which no one can foresee. No bureau, no commission, no leader and no despot can comprehend the future, much less mould and select it out of the infinite profusion of the human spirit. It is a spirit which like all of nature is much too mysterious and much too complex to be brought within the compass of any system of ideas and any set of rules.

That is why liberty is one of the conditions of human progress. Without it the dead hand of the past is forever upon the future, and our present ignorance is the enemy of our increasing enlightenment. No one in his senses supposes that the whole of human activity can be free. But it is the prejudice if you like, the proven faith I believe, of free men that the domain of liberty should be as wide as possible and that the domain of authority should be as limited as possible. And so, even when free men enlarge authority, as in the modern world they must, they do it in the knowledge that it is expedient and not glorious, that it is necessary but dangerous, that it is useful but costly. However much they may alter their methods, adapting them to new circumstances, it will continue to be their basic conviction that the state is the servant and not the master of the people.

INDEX

82 - 4729